ERP Magazine January–February 2019 – Issue 2

Disclaimer

Current Issue Contents

Previous Issue (Included)

- Taking Quick Input from Users with a Standard Function Module

- ALV Row Coloring: A Primer for SAP Developers

- A Simple Regular Expression Exercise

- Learn to Use Advanced Open SQL Features in SAP Reports for the HANA environment

- Using Debugger Standard Functions for Skipping as well as moving Back within Code

- A Little-Known Problem of the "FOR ALL ENTRIES IN" Construct

- Specifying Exporting and Returning Parameters for Functional Methods in SAP NetWeaver 7.50

- Debugging Applications after Modal Dialog Displayed

- Four Easy Coding Steps to Execute a Program in Background

- Learn to Determine Employee Locking Programmatically

- Learn to Find Whether a Payroll Area Is Locked for Maintenance

- How to Read Fixed Values of a Domain in Your Programs

- Distinctions between the Two Behaviors of the SUBMIT Statement

- Use the Two Variants of the CALL TRANSACTION Statement with Ease

- Setting Default Ranges for Selection Options upon Declaration

- Learn How to Determine if a Posting Date lies in an Open or Closed Period

Developing a Simple, User-Friendly SAPUI5 App in WebIDE Using Object List Items and Expression Binding

A lot is being discussed these days about Fiori and SAPUI5. It is a must for ABAP developers to learn how to develop SAPUI5 applications. In this article, we will learn to create a simple SAPUI5 application that will use expression binding in conjunction with the Object List Item control.

The main steps required for this are:

1 Open WebIDE. From the menu, choose File → New -- > Project from Template, as shown in Figure 1.

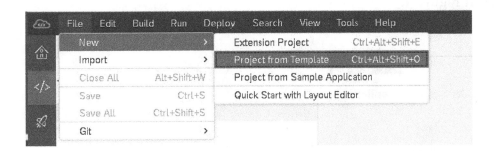

Figure 1: Create Project from Template

This will display the screen shown in Figure 2.

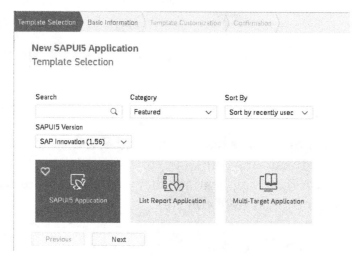

Figure 2: Specifying Template

Choose the SAPUI5 application and click the Next button. A dialog will appear, asking about the basic information of the new application we are about to create. There are two fields we must fill in: the Project Name and the Namespace. In this example, let's use ExpressionDemo as the value for both fields. We can see how this will look in Figure 3.

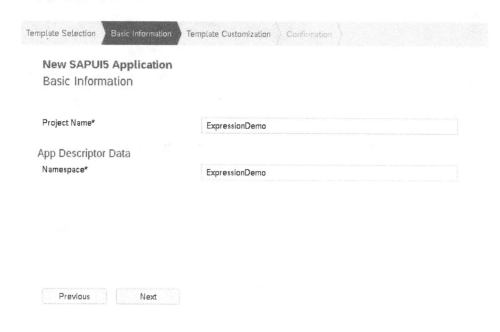

Figure 3: Basic Information

Click the Next button.

We will now be asked to enter the view name and the view type. Keep the view type as XML and set the view name as the default View1. Press the Finish button.

A confirmation message will appear, saying that the project ExpressionDemo will be created in our workspace (see Figure 4).

New SAPUI5 Application
Confirmation

A new project named ExpressionDemo will be created in your workspace.

Figure 4: Confirmation Message

Until this point, the application files will look like those shown in Figure 5.

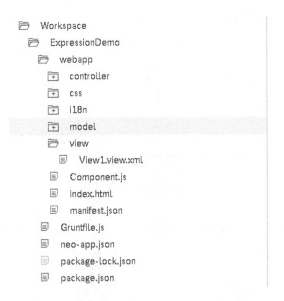

Figure 5: Application Files

Note the folder webapp, which contains the subfolders css, model and view, as well as the i18n folder. In the view folder, we can see View1.view.xml, which we have created. A manifest.json file appears, along with the index.html file.

To give the application a meaningful title, we now need to enter one in the folder. For this example, let's use "Residents list," as shown in Figure 6.

Figure 6: File i18n.properties

In order to program our application, we will now create a new file with the name Data.json. To do this, right click on the webapp folder and choose option New → File from the context menu that appears. A dialog will pop up, as shown in Figure 7.

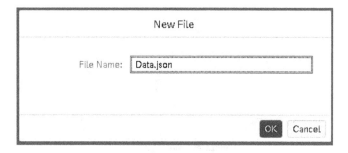

Figure 7: New File Dialog

Here, we will define mock data that will be displayed in our application.

```
{
"ResidentData": [ {
      "Person_Name": "John Mann",
      "Person_Age": "65"
}, {
      "Person_Name": "Samuel Fernandes",
      "Person_Age": "17"
}, {
      "Person_Name": "Jonathan Reed",
      "Person_Age": "88"
}, {
      "Person_Name": "Yvonne Davis",
```

```
        "Person_Age": "58"
},{

        "Person_Name": "Rebecca James",
        "Person_Age": "44"
},{

        "Person_Name": "Elizabeth White",
        "Person_Age": "61"
    }]
}
```

This file is addressed in the manifest.json file, as shown in Figure 8.

```
                                                                manifest.json ×  Gruntfile.js ×  View1.view.xml ×  index.html ×  Component.js ×
59              "type": "sap.ui.model.resource.ResourceModel",
60 ▾            "settings": {
61                  "bundleName": "ExpressionDemo.ExpressionDemo.i18n.i18n"
62              }
63          },
64 ▾        "DataResults": {
65              "type": "sap.ui.model.json.JSONModel",
66              "uri": "model/Data.json"
67          }
68      },
69 ▾    "resources": {
70 ▾        "css": [{
71              "uri": "css/style.css"
72          }]
73      },
```

Figure 8: File manifest.json

We will now create the view in which the Object List item is to be displayed. Here, the result of the expression binding will be shown.

```
<mvc:View
 controllerName="ExpressionDemo.ExpressionDemo.controller.View1"
   xmlns:html="http://www.w3.org/1999/xhtml"
   xmlns:mvc="sap.ui.core.mvc"
   displayBlock="true" xmlns="sap.m">

   <App id="idAppControl">
   <pages>
     <Page title="{i18n>title}">
       <content>
```

```
<List class="sapUiResponsiveMargin" width="auto"
    items="{DataResults>/ResidentData}">
    <items>
        <ObjectListItem title="{DataResults>Person_Name}"
            number="{DataResults>Person_Age}"
            numberUnit="Age"
            numberState="{= ${DataResults>Person_Age} >
            60 ? 'Success' : 'Error' }"/>
    </items>
</List>
</content>
</Page>
</pages>
</App>
</mvc:View>
```

The output of this code is shown here.

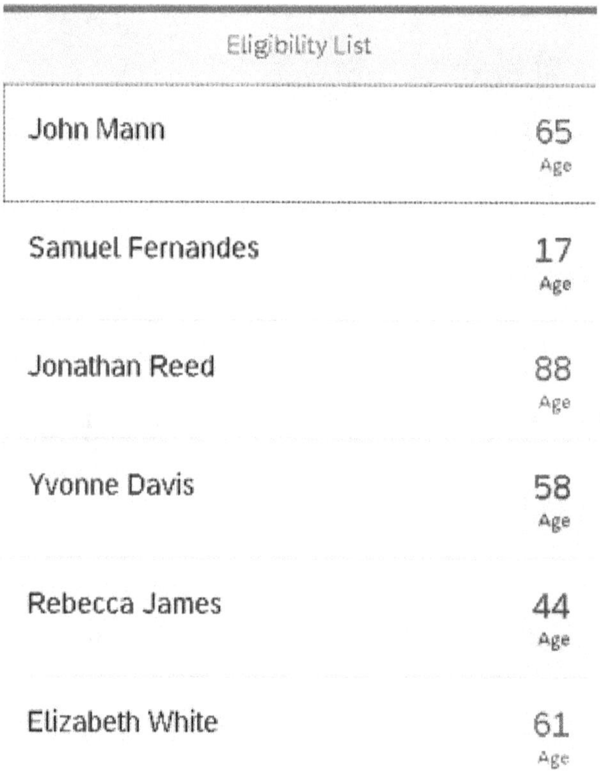

Eligibility List	
John Mann	65 Age
Samuel Fernandes	17 Age
Jonathan Reed	88 Age
Yvonne Davis	58 Age
Rebecca James	44 Age
Elizabeth White	61 Age

As you see, we have displayed a list in which a number of employee residents' names and ages appear. Depending on the age, the display colors differ.

Use the New NetWeaver 7.52 Console Output Function in ADT

Most people are not aware that in the new ADT (ABAP development tools) for NetWeaver 7.52, it is possible to execute a program in the console without the need for SAPGUI. This provides a quick way of testing code using the console output. In this article, we will see how to do this.

Consider the program shown in Figure 1.

```
▸ ⓟ ZST17_TEST1 ▸
1   *&-----------------------------------------------------------------*
2   *& Report zst17_test1
3   *&-----------------------------------------------------------------*
4   *&
5   *&-----------------------------------------------------------------*
6   REPORT zst17_test1.
7
8   write : / 'Console Output'.|
9
10
```

Figure 1: Example Program

With your cursor over the ABAP source code in Eclipse, right click to access the Context menu. Follow the menu path **Run as ABAP Application (Console)**. Alternately, you may use the key F9. The menu path is shown in Figure 2.

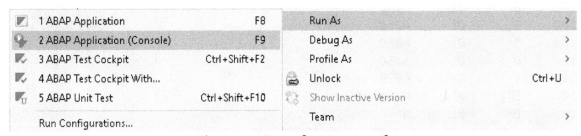

Figure 2: Console Menu path

This will open the output of the program in the ABAP console, as shown in Figure 3.

Figure 3: Console Output

Let us consider another example:

```
Select * from t512t into table @data(itab) up to 100 rows.
cl_demo_output=>display( itab ).
```

Here we have a simple program that uses a SELECT statement and then the DISPLAY method of the CL_DEMO_OUTPUT class. You can view the quick output of the method in the console by using the menu path mentioned earlier. The output is shown in Figure 4.

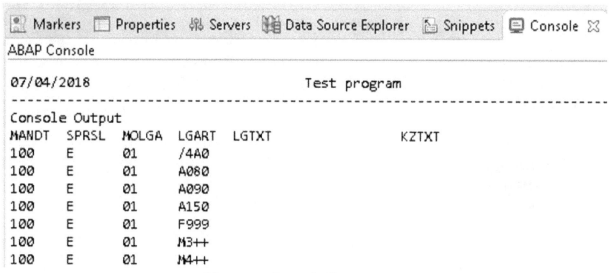

Figure 4: Console Output

As you see, in the console table, we have all the columns of the internal table ITAB. You can scroll to the right to see other columns in the table.

Demystifying the New UNION Command in Open SQL

In its newer releases, ABAP now supports the UNION command. This command allows you to merge the result sets of two separate SELECT queries into a single data set. In this article, we will see how we can use the UNION command and its variants in an ABAP program. Before this command was introduced, we used two separate SELECT queries to merge data sets, one using an INTO TABLE.. clause and the other using an APPENDING TABLE.. clause. These could be from two different tables or a single table.

Consider the following table contents:

CODE1	TEXT1
01	First
02	Second

Contents of Table ZTAB1

CODE2	TEXT2
02	Second
10	Tenth
20	Twentieth

Contents of Table ZTAB2

Imagine we require the union set of the rows of both these tables. Before the advent of the UNION command, we would have needed two separate SELECT statements to combine the data into one internal table. This would have looked like:

```
SELECT
   CODE1 AS CODE,
   TEXT1 AS TEXT
  FROM zTAB1
  INTO TABLE @DATA(myitab).

SELECT
```

```
        CODE2 AS CODE,
        TEXT2 AS TEXT
        FROM zTAB2
        APPENDING CORRESPONDING FIELDS OF @my_itab.
```

In newer releases such as NetWeaver 7.52, the UNION command can merge the data with one statement. An example of this is:

```
SELECT
    code1 AS code,
    text1 AS text
  FROM ztab1
UNION
    code2 AS code,
    text2 AS text
  FROM ztab2
INTO TABLE @DATA(myitab).
```

As you see, a single INTO clause can be used if the UNION command is included. The combined results after the union will be like those shown here:

CODE	TEXT
01	First
02	Second
10	Tenth
20	Twentieth

Contents of internal table MYITAB

In our example, the "02 – Second" entry exists in both the tables ZTAB1 and ZTAB2; however, only one entry appears in the combined result. By default, the UNION DISTINCT form applies, and any duplicates like this are removed from the final result set.

Now consider a scenario in which you need to include duplicate entries in the output internal table. For this, use the UNION ALL variant of the command. The code for this is:

```
SELECT
    code1 AS code,
    text1 AS text
  FROM ztab1
UNION ALL
    code2 AS code,
    text2 AS text
  FROM ztab2
INTO TABLE @DATA(myitab).
```

The output of this code is shown here:

CODE	TEXT
01	First
02	Second
02	Second
10	Tenth
20	Twentieth

Contents of internal table MYITAB

For further information, refer to the following link:

* https://help.sap.com/doc/abapdocu_752_index_htm/7.52/en-US/abapunion.htm

Make Your Own Modern-Style Fuzzy-Search-Based Field Value Help with Transaction SE11 – a Guide for SAP HANA Developers

In this article, we will see the new style of smart search help, based on a fuzzy search. Such search helps are displayed the moment the user starts writing within a field rather than when the user explicitly presses the F4 key. Moreover, this help may be used to search within a number of table columns rather than just a single column. For example, suppose we have a Code column along with a description. We need to search for Tax. This search could return entries like "Tax" in the Code field as well as "Tax wage type" in the description.

It is also possible to apply fuzzy search capability to searches. Suppose there a number of entries including the syllable "tax" in a given table (in this case, our selection method table T512T). However, in the field, if the user mistakenly enters "tex" rather than "tax," a traditional search function will not find the entries the user is looking for. With the new fuzzy-search-enabled search helps, you can set the error-tolerance factor so that slight mistakes are ignored and entries with similar spellings are found.

So let's understand what we need to create, and then we will look at the procedure. The search help values appear as you type in the input field rather than after pressing F4, as shown in Figure 1.

Wage Type	Wage Type Long Text
/200	AVB 00: Regard cont./NRS
MS00	T558A: /500
K002	Pool K001/590
K002	Topf K001/590
Y004	Original M004
Y006	Original M006
M500	Balance (P0011)
Z004	M004 difference
Z006	M006 difference
N100	100% non-taxable
Not all search results shown...	

Figure 1: Search Help

The basic procedure is the same as for normal search helps, but newer releases have an enhanced options block with a number of checkboxes, allowing you to enable the functionalities we have just covered.

Go to transaction SE11 and enter the name of the search help that you would like to create. Then create the button. In our case, we are using the value ZST17_SEARCH_HELP and the selection method T512t. The enhanced options block is shown in Figure 2.

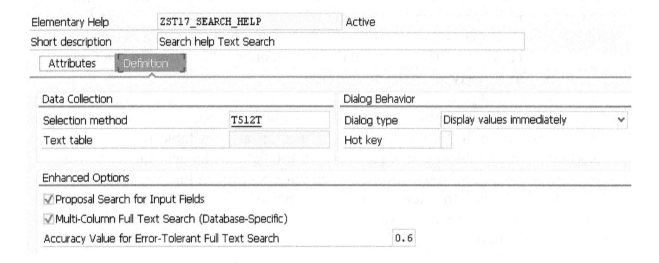

Figure 2: Enhanced Options Block

Suppose we have a search help based on the table T512t and two fields are included in the help. These are the LGART and LGTXT fields, as shown in Figure 3.

Figure 3: Fields LGART and LGTXT

We can include this help in our program using the following statement for a parameter field:

PARAMETERS lgart type t512t-lgart MATCHCODE OBJECT zst17_search_help.

The two checkboxes are of primary importance. The first checkbox (Proposal Search for Input Fields) must be ticked, so that once the user starts typing in the field, the proposed search help options start to appear automatically.

The second checkbox allows the user to search for the text entered in the field in the Wage Type code as well as in the description field, as shown in Figure 4.

Wage Type	Wage Type Long Text
TAXS	Student LoanOverride /402
TAX0	Taxation override /401
TAXR	Taxation override refund
TAXT	Taxation override termin
MTAX	Adjust Tax
BTAX	Tax on Bonus Amount
TADD	Additional Tax
/TAX	IncomeTax
TA30	Tax Arrs Ded (IT14 bal)
TA20	Tax Arrears Bal to Repay

Not all search results shown...

Figure 4: Search Results

Most importantly, we can set the accuracy value for error-tolerant full-text search help. Here, we can specify a value of accuracy for any errors in typing by the user. For example, a lower value means that we are tolerant of bigger errors. A value of 0.6 entered in this field is more tolerant of errors than a value of 0.8.

In my system, when I set the value as 0.8, the system accepted "tex" for the word "tax" and displayed the values shown in Figure 5.

Wage Type	Wage Type Long Text
/EXT	Prvt Hlth Ins. Extra Tax
YEXT	Total exemption on forms
/3TT	Exempted tax
M500	External Transfer
M830	External transfer
/47Z	Exch. rate gain tax
/Y7P	Gross.Exmpt.by TERL
M804	Training - external
/30I	Benefits TI-Extended
/41Z	Tax ex. ER-High Tech

Not all search results shown...

Figure 5: Error-Tolerant Search Results

Debugging SAPUI5 Applications with Ease – A Guide for Fiori Developers

No matter how good a developer you are, you will always need debugging tools. Working with SAPUI5 programming with WebIDE is no exception. In this article, we will discuss the steps for debugging any problems in your SAPUI5 applications. We will first make a simple application using WebIDE, and then we will debug it.

We will use Google Chrome developer tools to debug the JS and monitor the variables of the program. On the way, we will look at the various functions available in Chrome's developer tools. Before diving into debugging details, let us first make a small SAPUI5 application.

The sample application will take a number as input and, when the user presses the Square button, will calculate its square and display it in a message.

The application is defined in WebIDE as an SAPUI5 application. It has a view—View1—where we have defined an input field and a button as shown:

```
<mvc:View
controllerName="DebuggerTest.DebuggerTest.controller.View1"
xmlns:html="http://www.w3.org/1999/xhtml"
xmlns:mvc="sap.ui.core.mvc"
displayBlock="true" xmlns="sap.m">
<App id="idAppControl">
<pages>
  <Page title="Squaring Numbers">
   <content>
<Input placeholder="Enter number and press Square button "
id="num" width="30%"/>
      <Button text="Square" press="squareNumber" width="10%"/>
   </content>
  </Page>
 </pages>
</App>
</mvc:View>
```

We specify that pressing the Square button calls the function squareNumber. In the view controller, a method squareNumber is defined. The code for this method is:

```
sap.ui.define([ "sap/ui/core/mvc/Controller" ], function (Controller) {
"use strict";
return
Controller.extend("DebuggerTest.DebuggerTest.controller.View1", {
    squareNumber: function () {
        var num1 = parseInt(this.getView().byId("num").getValue());
        var square = num1 * num1;
        sap.m.MessageToast.show("Square is " + square);
    }
    });
});
```

When the application is run, a screen appears, as shown in Figure 1.

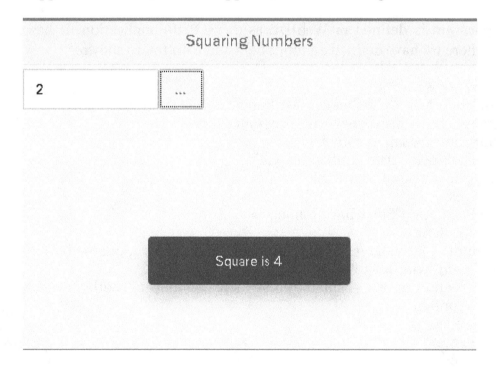

Figure 1: Application Screen

The user enters a number in the Number field and presses the Square button. The square is then displayed as a message.

And so, our app is up and running and ready to be debugged.

Now let's move on to the debugging. As I mentioned earlier, the debugger is one of Chrome's developer tools. There are two ways of opening the tools. One way is just to press the F12 key; alternately, you can right click within the browser and then choose the Inspect option on the right-hand side. This will open the Developer tools on the right, as shown in Figure 2.

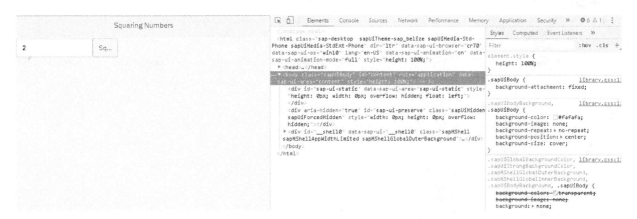

Figure 2: Developer Tools

Let us look at the main parts of the Chrome debugging tool panel.

- Elements: The element panel shows the SAPUI5 controls in HTML.

- Console: Any messages generated by the app will appear here. You can also type in the values of the variables addressed in the app and change them.

- Sources: Here you can see the source code of the app files. You can use this to set breakpoints within the code.

- Network: All resources used in the app are listed on this tab. This contains important information about the time it takes to load a particular resource. To find this information, go to the Network tab and press the F5 key. In the Network section, you can see the resource name and the time taken. If the resource loaded successfully, the status column will show 200; for an error, it will show code 400 or 500.

So, let's come back to our main point: how to set a breakpoint in your code.

Here are two ways of doing this.

Once the developer tools are open, select the Sources tab. The screen will look like the one shown in Figure 3.

Figure 3: Sources Tab

A tree will appear showing the list of files in your application. Double click the file that contains the code you would like to debug. In our case, we want to put a breakpoint at the function squareNumber that we have written. We will find this function in the View1.controller file. Double clicking this will display the source code of the file. Alternately, you can press CTRL+O to display a command field in which you can enter the View1.controller file name to go to the source code.

Once you have selected the file, the source code will be visible. To stop the code execution on a given line, click the line number. This will set a blue marker on the chosen line, as shown in Figure 4.

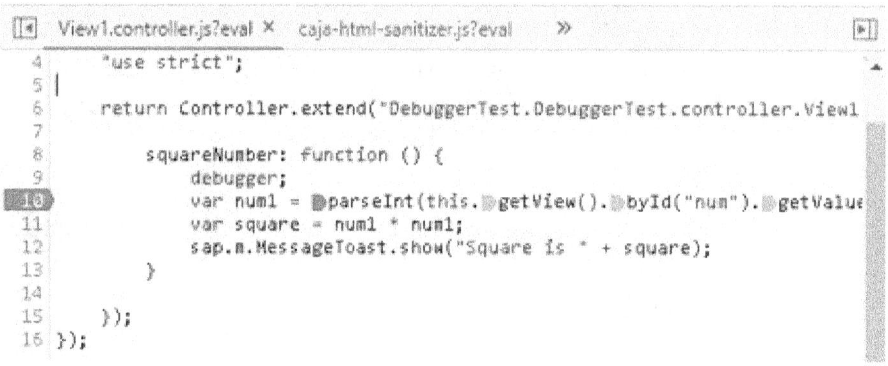

Figure 4: Selected Line

As you see, we have set the marker on line 10. We want the program to stop here at the time of execution.

When we reload the app in the browser, enter the value in the number field, and press the Square button, we will see that the code processing stops at line 10, where we have set the breakpoint. The line currently being executed is indicated by the highlighted box, as shown in Figure 5.

```
 1  sap.ui.define([
 2      "sap/ui/core/mvc/Controller"
 3  ], function (Controller) {
 4      "use strict";
 5
 6      return Controller.extend("DebuggerTest.DebuggerTest.controller.View1", {
 7
 8          squareNumber: function () {
 9
10              var num1 = parseInt(this.getView().byId("num").getValue());
11              var square = num1 * num1;
12              sap.m.MessageToast.show("Square is " + square);
13          }
14
15      });
16  });
```

Figure 5: The Line Being Executed

Setting a hard breakpoint is also possible in the JS code. To do this, we would write the debugger statement in the program code. When the user executes the application, the program will stop at the debugger statement. In this example, we have written the debugger statement within the squareNumber function. As you will see, the program execution stops, as shown in Figure 6.

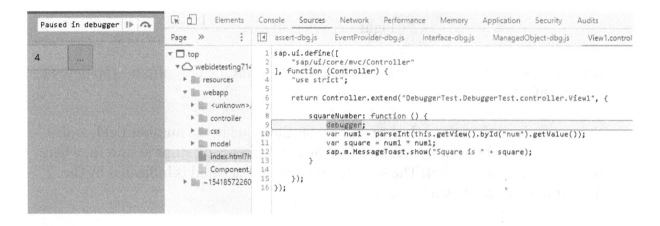

Figure 6: The Debugger Is Triggered

On the left side, the message "Paused in debugger" appears.

Checking and Changing Variable Values

Simply hovering the mouse over a variable will show its value, as shown in Figure 7.

```
    View1.controller.js?eval ×

1   sap.ui.define([
2       "sap/ui/core/mvc/Controller"
3   ], function (Controller) {
4       "use strict";
5
6       return Controller.extend("DebuggerTest.DebuggerTest.controller.View1", {
7
8           squareNumber: function () {
9               debugger;
10              var num1 = parseInt(this.getView().byId("num").getValue());    num1 = 2
11              var square = num1 * num1;
12              sap.m.MessageToast.show("Square is " + square);
13          }
14
15      });
16  });
```

Figure 7: Value Displayed

As you see, when we place the mouse cursor on the variable num1, a red box appears around it and the value 2 is displayed.

As you execute the program within the debugger line by line, the value of any variable used in the line will be shown at the end of the line (see Figure 8).

```
[◄]   assert-dbg.js    EventProvider-dbg.js    Interface-dbg.js    ManagedObject-dbg.js    View1.controller.js?eval ×

 1  sap.ui.define([
 2      "sap/ui/core/mvc/Controller"
 3  ], function (Controller) {
 4      "use strict";
 5
 6      return Controller.extend("DebuggerTest.DebuggerTest.controller.View1", {
 7
 8          squareNumber: function () {
 9              debugger;
10              var num1 = parseInt(this.getView().byId("num").getValue());    num1 = 4
11              var square = num1 * num1;   square = 16
12              sap.m.MessageToast.show("Square is " + square);
13          }
14
15      });
16  });
```

Figure 8: Variable Values Displayed

As you can see in the previous figure, the value of num1 is written at the end of the line after the execution of that line (line 10). Likewise, the value of the square, 16, is written at the end of line 11.

Here are the main keys used for progressing through the code:

Key	Purpose
F10	Step over next function call (used if you don't want to step into a function)
Shift + F11	Step out of current function
F11	Step into current function call
F8	Resume script execution, or stop at a breakpoint (or debugger statement)

To continue the execution of the application or to stop at the next breakpoint, press F8. If you want to go inside a function, press F11. To come back out of it, use Shift +F11.

The keys and icons used are the same for executing the code line by line or function by function. The line currently being executed is highlighted in blue, as shown in Figure 9.

```
 6        return Controller.extend("DebuggerTest.DebuggerTest.controller.View1", {
 7
 8            squareNumber: function () {
 9                debugger;
10                var num1 = parseInt (this. getView(). byId("num"). getValue( num1 = 2
11                var square = num1 * num1;
12                sap.m.MessageToast.show("Square is " + square);
13            }
14
```

Figure 9: Line Currently Being Executed

In the lower part of the screen, you will see the console window displayed. Here, we can check the variables within the program and also change their values. In order to check a variable's value, enter the name of the variable. Its value will then appear, and you can view it or change it. You can also carry out computations, in the form of expressions involving program variables.

Figure 10: Value of Variable num1

When you enter the expression as shown in Figure 10 and press Enter, the computed value will be displayed on the next line. For example, the parseInt function returns the value 2. We assigned x = num1, so x will have the value 2. We defined "c" in the console and assigned to it num1/3, which will have the value 0.6666.

```
> parseInt(this.getView().byId("num").getValue());
< 2
> x = num1
< 2
> c = num1 /3
< 0.6666666666666666
```

Figure 11: Calculations in the Console

We can change the values of the variables here as well. For example, in the console we have assigned the value 2 to num1.

We can also write evaluation expressions, such as num1 > 2. In this example, "false" appears, since num1 is not greater than 2, as shown in Figure 12.

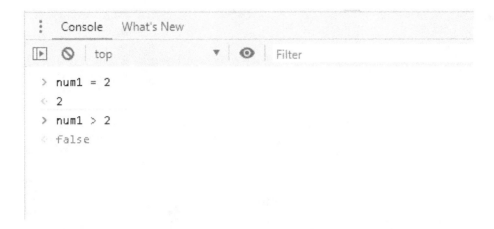

Figure 12: Evaluation Expression Result

Writing Conditional CASE.. ENDCASE Expressions within CDS Views – A Guide for HANA Developers

In this article, we will see how to write a simple CDS view that will use conditional CASE and ENDCASE expressions based on the values contained in the underlying table fields. Before defining this CDS view in detail, let us start with a requirement that we are going to solve.

Suppose we have to define a CDS view ZST17_2 based on the table T512t. The fields of the outputted CDS view must include SPRSL (language), Country Grouping (MOLGA), Wage Type (LGART), and Wage Type Description (LGTXT). We also need to include a new field for Country Text. The MOLGA should only be from 08 to 12, and importantly, the Country field we have introduced must show as USA when the MOLGA is equal to 10. In all other cases, we will output "Rest of the World." For this condition, we will use the CASE expression.

Another requirement is that rows with blank text for the Wage Type Description must be excluded.

The CDS view fulfilling these requirements is shown here:

```
@AbapCatalog.sqlViewName: 'ZST17_22'
@AbapCatalog.compiler.compareFilter: true
@AccessControl.authorizationCheck: #CHECK

define view ZST17_2 as select from t512t {
  key t512t.sprsl as Sprsl,
  key t512t.lgart as Wage_Type ,
  key t512t.molga as Molga,
  case t512t.molga
    when '10' then 'USA'
    else 'Rest of World'
  end as Country,
  t512t.lgtxt as Wage_Type_Description
}
where sprsl = 'E'
and not lgtxt = ' '
and ( molga between '08' and '12' )
```

This selects the fields SPRSL, LGART, and MOLGA from table T512t. We have used the CASE.. ELSE.. END expression to output "USA" when the value of MOLGA is equal to 10 and to output "Rest of the World" in all other cases. The comparison is based on the MOLGA field of table T512T (t512t.molga), and the header of this field is Country. For LGTXT, we have used the NOT operator to exclude any blank values. The LGTXT is outputted as Wage_type_description.

The output of the CDS view will look like the one shown in Figure 1.

SPRSL	WAGE_TYPE	MOLGA	COUNTRY	WAGE_TYPE_DESCRIPTION
E	B210	10	USA	Dental ER contribution
E	BC31	10	USA	EE age catch-up contrib
E	BU31	10	USA	ER age catch-up contrib
E	MC04	10	USA	MC OASDI (employer)
E	MC06	10	USA	MC Medicare (employer)
E	MCOR	10	USA	Claim of right
E	/001	11	Rest of World	Valuation basis 1
E	/002	11	Rest of World	Valuation basis 2
E	/003	11	Rest of World	Valuation basis 3
E	/02A	11	Rest of World	Frozen averages
E	/105	11	Rest of World	Working net pay

Figure 1: Program Output

As you see, the field language, wage type code, and country group are displayed, along with the wage type description and country name. For the MOLGA value of 10, the country is displayed as "USA," while for 11 (and other similar values), the country field shows "Rest of World."

Mastering the New CEIL and FLOOR Functions in ABAP

In recent releases, ABAP has introduced a number of new arithmetic functions. In this short piece, we will see how to use the new functions CEIL and FLOOR in our programming. Before seeing a working example of CEIL and FLOOR, let us briefly define them:

- CEIL(r) – This returns the smallest integer that is larger than the integer R passed as an argument.
- FLOOR(r) – This returns the largest integer value that is smaller than the integer R.

Now, consider this simple working example:

```
data int1 type p decimals 2.
data int2 type p decimals 2.
data temp type p DECIMALS 2.

temp =  111 / 2.

int1  = ceil( temp ) .
write int1 .

skip.
int2 = floor( temp ) .
write int2 .
```

Here, we have defined the integers int1 and int2, along with a temp, as all having decimals 2. We have divided 111 by 2 and stored the answer as 55.5. However, after applying the CEIL, this value gets rounded off to 56.00, and this is stored in INT1. Likewise, when the FLOOR is applied on the temp (in this case, 55.5), this is rounded down to 55 and stored in INT2. The output of the program is shown in Figure 1.

int1 is 56.00
int2 is 55.00

Figure 1: Program Output

Creating Your First Very Simple OData SAP Gateway Service

Contributed by www.ERPWorkbench.com

With so much information available about developing mobile and responsive applications within SAP at the moment and so many new technologies appearing, it can be very difficult to know where to start. So, Fiori is the future—along with SAPUI5? What about the SAP Gateway and OData, or even HANA, and the endless list of other names and technologies around? How do these all fit into the big picture for an SAP developer?

Let's start at the ground level, the NetWeaver Gateway, where traditional SAP ABAP skills are required as part of building a Fiori app. The SAP Gateway has actually been around for many years, but with the move to Fiori/mobile/responsive apps, it is being used more and more and is now a key part of the SAP landscape. The Gateway allows data within your SAP system(s) to be accessed by the outside world via OData services.

Steps Required to Create OData Service

In this new Fiori world, the front end is created using SAPUI5 with the Web IDE. This calls an OData service on the SAP system via the SAP Gateway. The OData service then uses ABAP to retrieve SAP data and returns it.

The example below will show you how to quickly create your first OData Gateway service using basic ABAP code to select data from a standard table.

1 Go to **SAP NetWeaver Gateway Service Builder,** transaction SEGW, where you will be able to build your service, as shown in Figure 1.

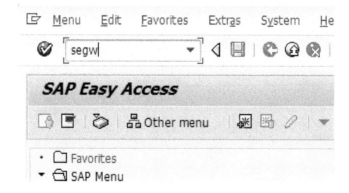

Figure 1: Transaction SEGW

Using the Create button (see Figure 2), create a project to store all your data models, implementations, entity types, entity sets, etc. (Don't worry too much about the terminology at this stage; all will become clear.)

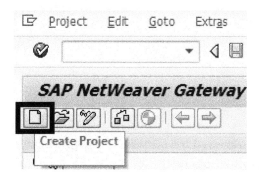

Figure 2: Create Project Button

We will now enter the project details, as shown in Figure 3. Enter a name, description, and package. Leave everything else as the default unless you know you need something specific. Then press Enter.

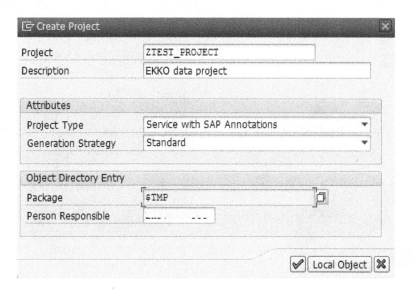

Figure 3: Create Project Dialog

2 We are going to base this example on a subset of the standard SAP table EKKO. In the newly created project, right click on the Data Model node and select **Import->DDIC Structure**, as shown in Figure 4.

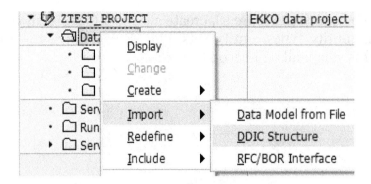

Figure 4: Import DDIC Structure

Enter EKKO in the ABAP structure field, along with an object name. In this example, we will use "purchaseorder." This is shown in Figure 5.

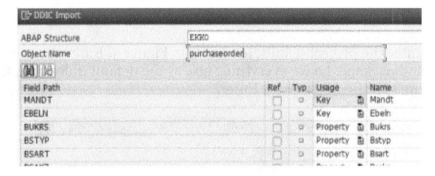

Figure 5: ABAP Structure EKKO

Expand the newly created node **Entity Type->purchaseorder** (shown in the left pane) and double click the Properties node. This is shown in Figure 6.

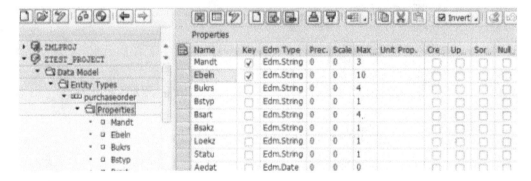

Figure 6: Entity Type "purchaseorder" Fields

We are only going to use the top few fields, so select all the fields below Status and delete them, as shown in Figure 7.

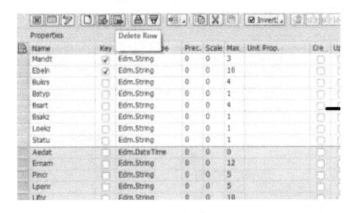

Figure 7: Deleting Rows

After the deletion, the entity type should look like the one in Figure 8.

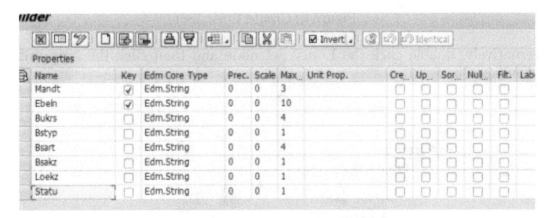

Figure 8: Fields after Deletion

Note: The reason we are not using all the fields is that some are incompatible with a gateway service unless you first change the data type. Later in this article, we will see where you would eventually get an error if you had used all the fields. This info might help you understand the error more quickly if you do create one in the future.

3 To create the entity set, right click on the Entity Set node and select Create (see Figure 9).

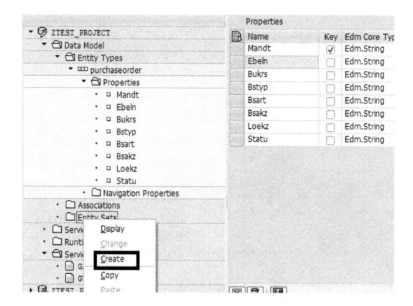

Figure 9: Create Entity Set

Alternatively, double click the Entity Set node and then click the **Append Row** button (see Figure 10).

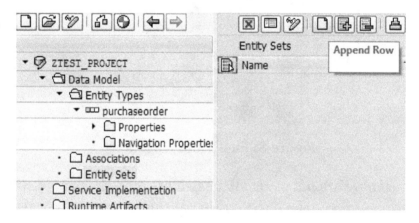

Figure 10: Append Row

Give the entity set a name (usually a plural of the entity type). Here, we will use "purchaseorders," as shown in Figure 11.

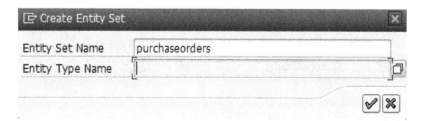

Figure 11: Create Entity Set

Select the entity type "purchaseorders" from the Selection Input Help, as shown in Figure 12.

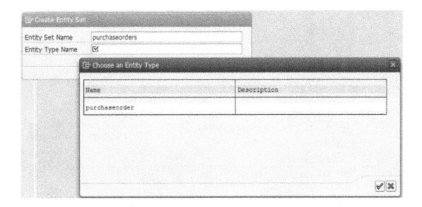

Figure 12: Entity Set Details

Once the entity type is selected, press Continue (the green tick). The entity set has now been created. It should appear under Entity Sets (see Figure 13).

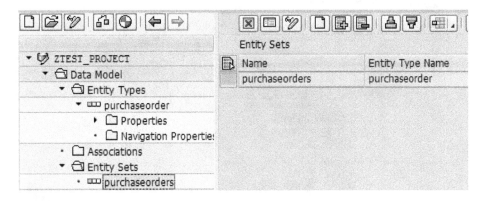

Figure 13: Entity Set "purchaseorders"

Double click the Project node (as shown in Figure 14) and generate the whole project using the **Generate Runtime Objects** button.

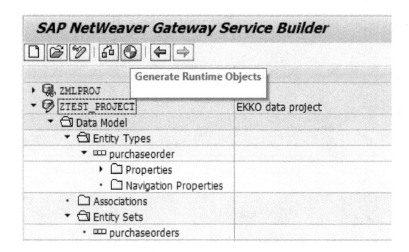

Figure 14: Generate Runtime Objects

You will now notice that service implementation objects have been created: Create, Delete, GetEntity (Read), GetEntitySet (Query), and Update, as shown in Figure 15.

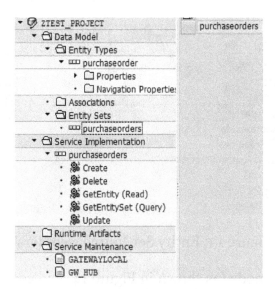

Figure 15: Generated Objects

4 Go to transaction /IWFND/MAINT_SERVICE. I always find I can only get this working if I add /n at the start, i.e., /n/IWFND/MAINT_SERVICE, as shown in Figure 16.

Figure 16: Transaction for Maintaining Service

Within /IWFND/MAINT_SERVICE, click the **Add Service** button, as shown in Figure 17.

Figure 17: Adding Service

Then, enter the information of the service you want to add. Notice you can use wildcards at this point to find your service, as shown in Figure 18.

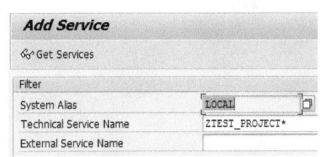

Figure 18: Entering Service Name

Press Enter to find the service or services that match your search criteria. Once they appear, click on the one you want to add, as shown in Figure 19.

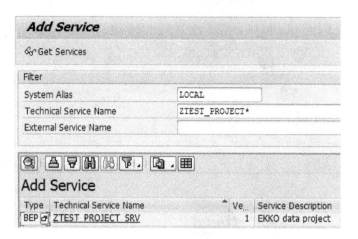

Figure 19: Finding Service

The next screen shows you the selected service details. Enter package details (i.e., local object), and leave everything as default, as shown in Figure 20.

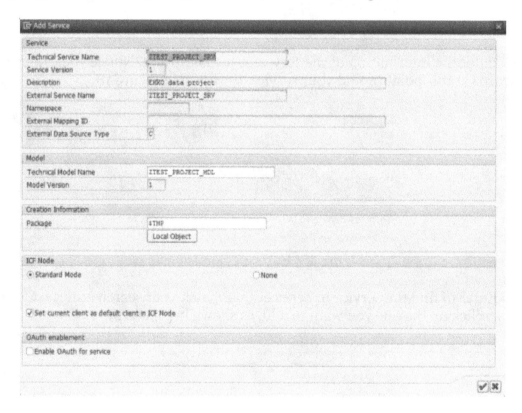

Figure 20: Entering Service Details

Then press the Okay button (the green tick).

You should now receive a popup message saying that your service "was created and its metadata was loaded successfully," as you see in Figure 21.

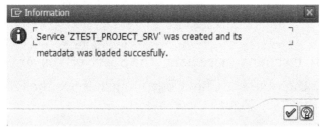

Figure 21: Success Message

Return to the previous page by clicking the Return button.

This will bring you back to the service catalog. Depending on how many services you have set up in your system, you may need to use the filter functionality to find your newly added service (see Figure 22).

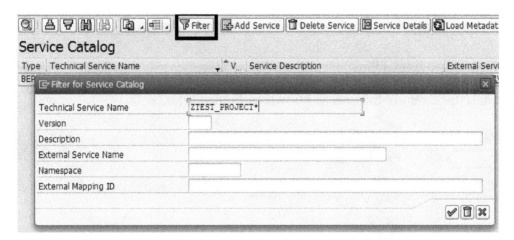

Figure 22: Filter Functionality

You should now see the service setup details and a green traffic light next to the ODATA ICF node in the bottom left-hand corner (see Figure 23).

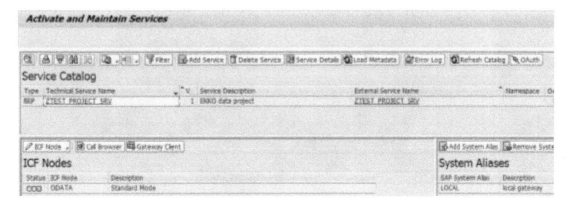

Figure 23: Service Catalog

5 We now need to test our service using the SAP NetWeaver Gateway Client, which is accessed via the Gateway Client button just above the ODATA node in the bottom left-hand corner (see Figure 24).

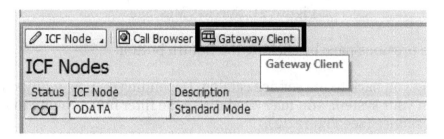

Figure 24: Testing Gateway Client

Here, leave Request URI as
/sap/opu/odata/sap/ZTEST_PROJECT_SRV/?$format=xml , which is the default, simply click the Execute button, as shown in Figure 25.

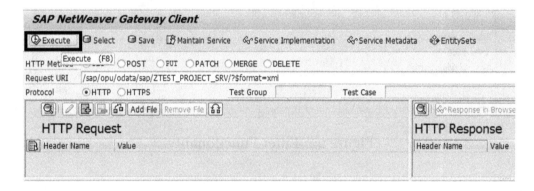

Figure 25: Executing the Service

You should then get an HTTP response with a green status code, as shown in Figure 26.

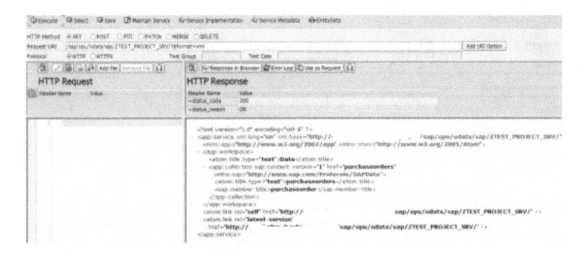

Figure 26: HTTP Response

Now, modify the URL so it ends with "$metadata?sap-ds-debug=true" and press Execute again, so we can return metadata properties of the purchaseorder entity, as shown in Figure 27.

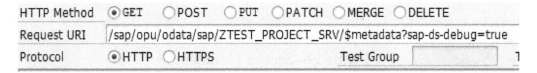

Figure 27: Metadata URI

The HTTP response, in this case showing the metadata, is shown in Figure 28.

Figure 28: Service Metadata

6 Now change the URI to end with "/purchaseorders?sap-ds-debug=true" so that we can target the data of the entity set purchaseorders (see Figure 29). The URI will become:

...."/sap/opu/odata/sap/ZTEST_PROJECT3_SRV/purchaseorders?sap-ds-debug=true"

Figure 29: Purchase Orders URI

When you press Execute, you should get the error shown in Figure 30, as we have not implemented the method that populates this data yet.

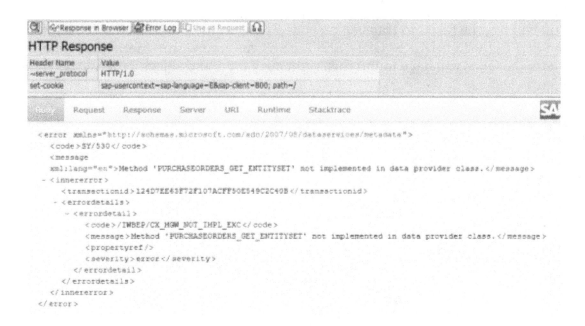

Figure 30: HTTP Error

6 Next, we need to implement the GetEntitySet method. For this, return to the SEGW transaction and find the service implementation methods you created before. Find the one called GetEntitySet (Query) and right click on it. Then, from the Context menu, select Go to ABAP Workbench, as shown in Figure 31.

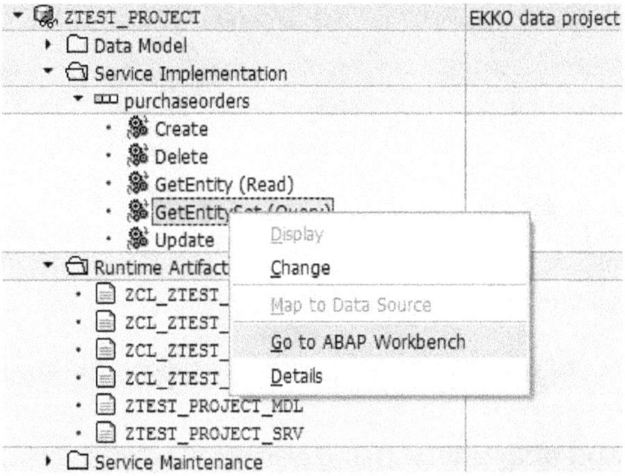

Figure 31: GetEntitySet Method

A message will appear saying the operation has not yet been implemented. Simply click OK to continue.

You will now be taken to transaction code SE80. In the object list on the left, find the PURCHASEORDERS_GET_ENTITYSET method within Methods->Inherited Methods. Once you have found this, right click on it and select Redefine, as shown in Figure 32.

Figure 32: Redefine Method

Within the method code that appears, simply add the SELECT statement shown in Figure 33.

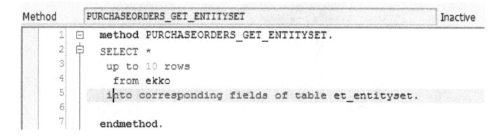

Figure 33: Coding GetEntitySet Method

Save the statement and activate it.

You may test your service again using the steps shown earlier. Change the URI to "/sap/opu/odata/sap/ZTEST_PROJECT_SRV/purchaseorders?sap-ds-debug=true" as shown in Figure 34.

<!-- Execute Select Save Maintain Service Service Implementation Service M -->
<!-- HTTP Method: GET POST PUT PATCH MERGE DELETE -->
<!-- Request URI: /sap/opu/odata/sap/ZTEST_PROJECT_SRV/purchaseorders?sap-ds-debug=true -->
<!-- Protocol: HTTP HTTPS   Test Group   Test Case -->
<!-- Add File Remove File -->

Figure 34: Purchase Orders URI

This time, some data should be returned, as shown in Figure 35.

Figure 35: Purchase Order Data

Remember that earlier in the article, I mentioned not using all the fields from the EKKO table, as some are not compatible. If you had included them all when executing the URI "/sap/opu/odata/sap/ZTEST_PROJECT_SRV/purchaseorders?sap-ds-debug=true", you would have received the error message shown in Figure 36.

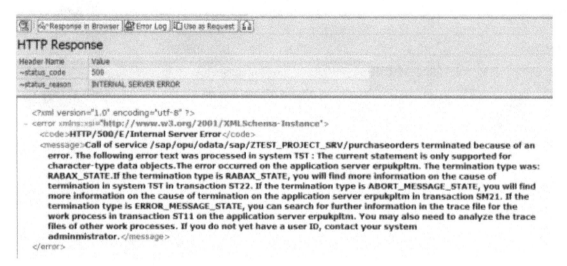

Figure 36: HTTP Error

Concluding Remarks

In this article we have covered the main steps in creating an OData service. The next step is to access this gateway service from your SAP Fiori App.

Using the New "Group By" Clause for Internal Table Control-Level Processing – Get Ready for the New Generation of ABAP Programming

Since NetWeaver 7.40, ABAP has provided a new GROUP BY clause for use with internal table loops. It can be used in a variety of forms. In this short article, we will review the use of the GROUP BY clause and groups in control-level processing. We will see how to calculate totals based on groups formed on a particular field.

Suppose we have a simple internal table with two fields, TEAM and POINTS. The contents of this internal table are shown in Figure 1.

TEAM	POINTS
Second Team	10
First Team	20
First Team	25
Second Team	15
First Team	11
Second Team	23

Figure 1: Contents of Internal Table SCORE_TABLE

For your reference, the definition of the table is:

```
TYPES: BEGIN OF SINGLE_ROW,
    TEAM TYPE C LENGTH 19,
    POINTS TYPE I,
    END OF SINGLE_ROW.

DATA SCORE_TABLE TYPE STANDARD TABLE OF SINGLE_ROW
    WITH KEY TEAM POINTS.
...
```

So, the internal table SCORE_TABLE has two fields, TEAM and POINTS. Our simple requirement is to display the total points of each team along with their names. This means there should be only two lines printed, as shown in Figure 2.

First Team Total	56
Second Team Total	48

Figure 2: Printed Output of Team Totals

The code that deals with this requirement is:

```
DATA TEAM_TOTAL TYPE SINGLE_ROW.

LOOP AT SCORE_TABLE ASSIGNING FIELD-SYMBOL(<ROW>)
     GROUP BY <ROW>-TEAM ASCENDING.
 CLEAR TEAM_TOTAL.

 LOOP AT GROUP <ROW> INTO DATA(TEMP_DATA).
   CONCATENATE TEMP_DATA-TEAM 'Total' INTO
   TEAM_TOTAL-TEAM SEPARATED BY SPACE.
    TEAM_TOTAL-POINTS = TEMP_DATA-POINTS +  TEAM_TOTAL-POINTS.
 ENDLOOP.
 WRITE :/ TEAM_TOTAL-TEAM , TEAM_TOTAL-POINTS.
ENDLOOP.
```

We use the GROUP BY clause in the outer loop and specify that the grouping will be based on the TEAM field (which is to be processed in ascending order). We have assigned this to the field symbol <ROW>. The outer loop is run once for each of the groups that have been identified in the internal table – in this case, twice, for "First Team" and "Second Team."

The inner loop runs for all rows in the table that contain the group currently being iterated (in our case, First Team or Second Team). The inner loop is run on all table rows, in the sequence of the group elements (i.e., First Team, Second Team, and so on). Within this loop, the team points and text are available; the contents of each row processed in the inner loop are stored in TEMP_DATA. As you can see, earlier we defined TEAM_TOTAL as having the same structure as the row type of the internal table SCORE_TABLE. This structure will serve to display the final totals.

In the inner loop, we concatenate the word "Total" with the team name and store it in the TEAM field of the structure TEAM_TOTAL. For the points, we total the points stored in TEMP_DATA-POINTS and store it in the structure field TEAM_TOTAL-POINTS. This is then displayed in TEAM_TOTAL outside the inner loop.

Once the inner loop is done, the outer loop is executed for the next group element (i.e., Second Team), followed by the inner loop for all rows in the table where the field TEAM equals "Second Team". Before the inner loop runs, we clear the contents of TEAM_TOTAL and the summation values so that the next team total can be correctly calculated. With this looping, we have now programmed control-level processing. The output of the program will be similar to the one shown in Figure 2.

Use the New "FOR" Loop for Populating Rows in Internal Tables – Modernize Your ABAP Code and Stand Out from the Crowd

Since NetWeaver 7.40, we have a new FOR loop that can be used to populate internal table rows. In this article, we will see a fully working example of the use of the FOR loop in conjunction with the VALUE expression.

Consider a simple internal table definition:

```
TYPES: BEGIN OF SINGLE_ROW,
    TEAM TYPE C LENGTH 19,
    POINTS TYPE I,
    END OF SINGLE_ROW.

DATA SCORE_TABLE TYPE STANDARD TABLE OF SINGLE_ROW
    WITH KEY TEAM POINTS.

SCORE_TABLE = VALUE #(
  FOR c = 1 UNTIL c > 4
  ( TEAM = 'Second Team'
    POINTS = c
    )
  ( TEAM = 'First Team '
    POINTS = 10 * c
    ) ).
```

Here we have an internal table with the name SCORE_TABLE, having two fields, TEAM and POINTS. We use the VALUE expression with a # to populate values in the internal table SCORE_TABLE. We have specified a counter C starting from 1 and looping until the value of C becomes larger than 4.

The FOR loop is executed four times. We start from 1, as c is equal to 1, and then go on, stopping before the value of C becomes greater than 4 – i.e., the loop runs from 1 to 4. For each loop pass, we add the row of Second Team, followed by a row of First Team having a value of 10 multiplied by the value of c. So, on the first loop pass, the contents of the internal table SCORE_TABLE are:

TEAM	POINTS
Second Team	1
First Team	10

At the end of the code, eight rows have been added and the contents are:

TEAM	POINTS
Second Team	1
First Team	10
Second Team	2
First Team	20
Second Team	3
First Team	30
Second Team	4
First Team	40

There are a total of eight rows in the table after the execution of the code.

Learn to Create Navigation Lists in Web Dynpro for ABAP Applications

While developing Web Dynpro for applications, developers may be required to provide easy navigation options for users – typically in a hierarchical format. One of the supported WD4A UI elements that may be used to display data in a sophisticated format is the navigation list. With this, developers can present data in an easy-to-use navigation form.

The aim of this article is to provide a primer on the navigation list and its advantages, as well as the main steps in integrating them into a fresh Web Dynpro application. For our purposes here, we will assume that the reader has basic knowledge of ABAP Objects and Web Dynpro.

Navigation List: An Overview

The navigation list lets developers display information in a tree-type format. A typical example is shown in Figure 1.

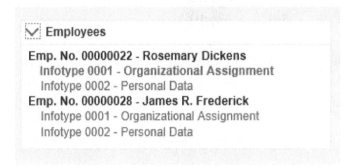

Figure 1: Navigation List Output

Optionally, this may include a title (in our case, it is "Employees"). Next to the title is an expandable icon (down arrow). This is used to hide the full navigation list. When collapsed, this will look like the one shown in Figure 2.

Figure 2: Navigation List Collapsed

The navigation list may contain a number of higher-level or top-level nodes (in our case, Employee 00000022 and Employee 00000028). Each high-level node may or may not contain a number of child nodes. In our example, these are shown as infotype names.

Note: The data nodes of a navigation list cannot be collapsed or expanded individually. Only the entire list can be collapsed or expanded.

By double clicking a child node, it is possible to view its details, for example if you want to view further information pertaining to the selected record. However, this may require writing a few lines of additional code.

Before diving into the details, let us first see the steps for displaying a navigation list.

- Creating the context for the navigation list, i.e., defining the recursive node in the context.

- Creating the navigation list UI element within the Web Dynpro view (specifying various property settings and linking the navigation list with the recursive node).

- Coding the methods that will populate the context node linked to the navigation list.

- Writing optional code for responding to the choosing of items shown in the navigation list.

Creating a Navigation List in a Web Dynpro Component

For the sake of this example, we will not look at the basic steps for creating a Web Dynpro component; we will assume that it is already in place. We are only considering the navigation list steps here.

We first need to create a context node corresponding to the navigation list we want. For this node, we will create a recursive child node. This lets us organize our data hierarchically. The child node has the same structure as its parent. The higher nodes are based on the parent node of the context (in our case, this will be MYLIS). On the other hand, the level-two nodes (child nodes) are based on the recursive nodes.

For this example, our Web Dynpro component in which the navigation list is to be embedded will be ZDEMO_NAVIGATION_LIST.

Let us now see how this is done.

1 Call transaction SE80, and make sure that the component is in edit mode. Click the component controller node to display the relevant component controller tabs on the right side. Select the Context tab. Right click the Context root node, and from the menu that appears, select the **Create Node** option. This will display the dialog box for node creation.

The typical settings for this node are shown in Figure 1.

Property	Value	
Nodes		
Node Name	NAV_NODE	
Interface Node		☐
Input Element (Ext.)		☐
Dictionary structure		
Cardinality	0..n	🖹
Selection	0..1	🖹
Initialization Lead Selection		☐
Singleton		☐
Supply Function		

Figure 1: Property Settings for Context Node

Enter a name for the node, then unselect the singleton property. Ensure that the cardinality of the node is set as 1..N or 0..N.

We will now specify attributes of the node. Right click the node and choose the **Create Attribute** menu option. We must define a number of attributes, starting with the node TEXT for storing the text to be displayed. Next, define the attribute SELECT_ENABLED, an indicator that allows you to determine whether the item may be selected or not.

The TEXT attribute is shown in Figure 2.

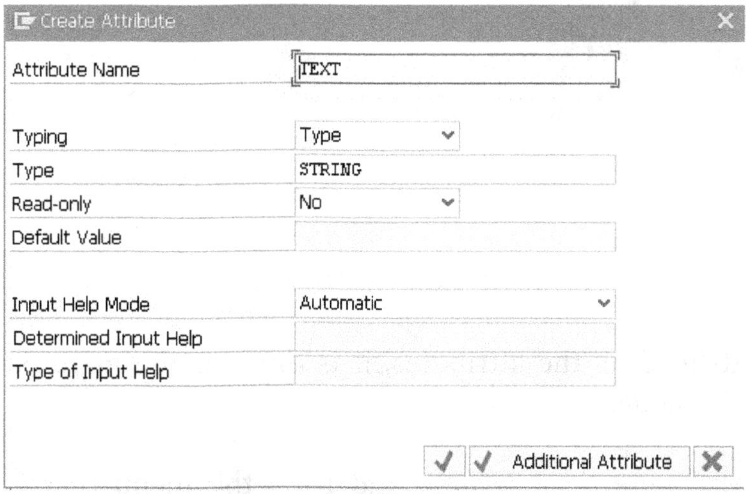

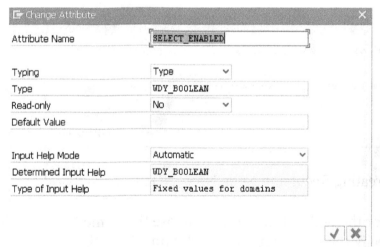

Figure 2: Text Attribute

The SELECT_ENABLED attribute is shown in Figure 3.

Figure 3: Attribute SELECT_ENABLED

In our case, we will also define a few fields that will be used to identify particular items in the list. Based on this, we will select further data from the database based on the selection.

Let's define INFTY and PERNR nodes, denoting the infotype and the employee number respectively. The context will look like the one shown in Figure 4.

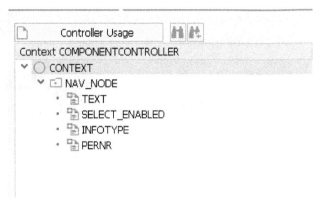

Figure 4: Context NAV_NODE

When we have defined all the attributes, it is time for the main part of this step: creating a recursive node.

Right click on the node NAV_NODE, and from the menu that appears, choose option Create Recursion Node. This will display a dialog box like the one shown in Figure 5.

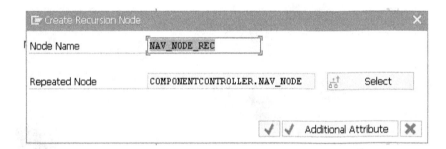

Figure 5: Creating Recursion Node NAV_NODE_REC Based on NAV_NODE

Enter a name for the node. Here, we will choose the name NAV_NODE_REC. Next, we need to specify the node (repeated node) on which the recursive node is based. Click the Select button and choose NAV_NODE.

The context node will look like the one shown in Figure 6.

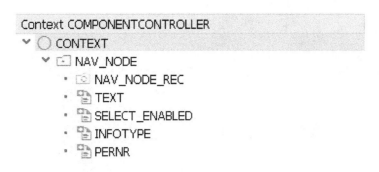

Figure 6: Context and Properties

2 The next step is to create a navigational list UI element within the view on which the validation list is to be displayed. In edit mode, double click the relevant view node. This will display the respective view in the right pane. In the main view, select the Context tab. Then, use the drag-and-drop feature to copy the component controller NAV_NODE to the Context MAIN of the view, as shown in Figure 7.

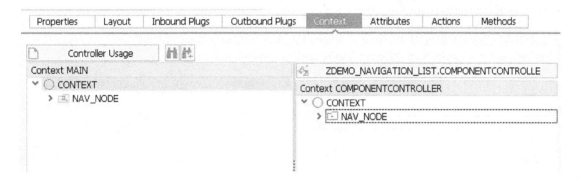

Figure 7: Context Node NAV_NODE

Select the Layout tab. The View Layout editor will open. Right click ROOTUIELEMENTCONTAINER and select the Insert UI element. A dialog box as shown in Figure 8 will appear.

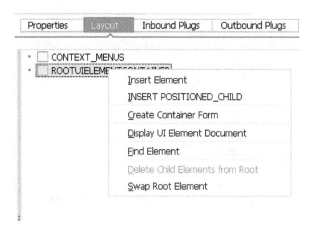

Figure 8: Insert Element

This will bring up a popup box as shown in Figure 9.

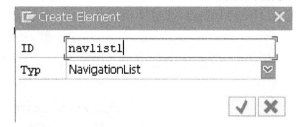

Figure 9: Creating UI Element NavigationList

Enter a suitable name for the element. Choose Navigation List as the type, and press Enter.

Now we need to link the newly created UI element with the context we created earlier. To do this, we need to set a number of settings for our navigation UI element.

- The itemSource property has to be set as root node NAV_NODE, which we defined earlier. Make sure you do not use the recursive node but the parent node.
- The itemText property determines the text that is displayed in the nodes of the navigation list. We will bind this property with the TEXT field of the context node.
- The itemSelectable property can be selected, depending on the requirement. If you want to give the user the option of displaying the detail of a particular element of the navigation list, select this.

The settings will look like those shown in Figure 10.

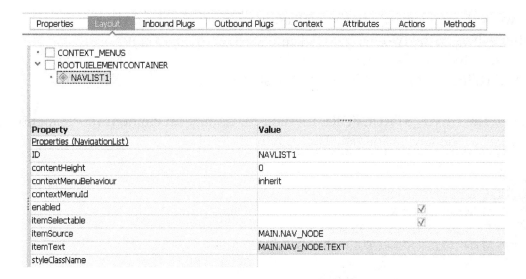

Figure 10: View Editor and Property Settings of Navigation List

3 The most important part comes next. We need to write appropriate code for populating data in the context in order to display the navigation list. This code can be written in the WDDOINIT method of the respective view.

Declaring Necessary Variables

First, define a number of variables that will be used for populating the context nodes. This code is shown here:

```
DATA P_MYNAVLIST TYPE WD_THIS->ELEMENT_NAV_NODE.
DATA P_NODE_NAVI_LIST TYPE REF TO IF_WD_CONTEXT_NODE.
DATA P_ELEMENT_NAVI_LIST TYPE REF TO IF_WD_CONTEXT_ELEMENT.
DATA P_NODE_RECURSION TYPE REF TO IF_WD_CONTEXT_NODE.
```

As you see, we have declared variables relevant to the parent node, the recursive node, and the element.

Creating Context Elements for Level-One Nodes

Next, we need to populate the data that is to be displayed. This means populating the higher nodes. We will use the top node specified earlier. Call the GET_CHILDNODE method using WD_CONTEXT to access a link to MYNAV.

```
P_NODE_NAVI_LIST = WD_CONTEXT->GET_CHILD_NODE( NAME =
        WD_THIS->WDCTX_NAV_NODE ).
```

Next, we will add elements to the collection of the node MYNAV. We need to assign suitable values to the two fields TEXT and PERNR. If you do not want the top nodes to be selected, make sure the value of SELECTION_ENABLED is set to ABAP_FALSE. Assign suitable text to the structure mynavlist.

Now, call the BIND_STRUCTURE method for adding an element (corresponding to mynavlist) to the navigation list. The code is shown here:

```
CLEAR P_MYNAVLIST.
P_MYNAVLIST-TEXT
  = 'Emp. No. 00000022 - Rosemary Dickens'.
P_MYNAVLIST-SELECT_ENABLED = ABAP_true.
P_MYNAVLIST-infotype   = ''.
P_MYNAVLIST-pernr = '00000022' .

P_ELEMENT_NAVI_LIST   = P_NODE_NAVI_LIST->BIND_STRUCTURE(
            NEW_ITEM          = P_MYNAVLIST
            SET_INITIAL_ELEMENTS = ABAP_FALSE ).
```

Here, we have added a single row (element) to the navigation list's node collection. This block of code must be called within a loop, so that we can add a number of top-level nodes. Inside the loop, use AT NEW to add a single row for one common value. For example, in our scenario, we must make sure that for all entries in the data table with a common employee number (such as 22), a single parent node is added. The parent node will have a number of child nodes showing infotypes.

For each top-level node, we now need to add child nodes (i.e., the nodes with infotype numbers and descriptions). In this case, we will get the reference for the context node to which the child nodes are to be added, using the method GET_CHILD_NODE.

```
P_NODE_RECURSION =
    P_ELEMENT_NAVI_LIST->GET_CHILD_NODE( NAME = 'NAV_NODE_REC' ).
```

In our example, we need to make sure the name of the recursive node is written in quotes (''). The above statement must be contained within the AT NEW or ON CHANGE OF command (from Step 2). This ensures we are adding the correct element as the parent node.

We then add child nodes to the element, using the BIND_STRUCTURE method. We first assign appropriate values to the structure P_MYNAVLIST, including text and employee number. For the SET_INITIAL_ELEMENTS parameter, we pass FALSE.

```
P_MYNAVLIST-select_enabled = ABAP_TRUE.
P_MYNAVLIST-INFoTYpe    = '0001'.
P_MYNAVLIST-text    = 'Infotype 0001 - Organizational Assignment'.
P_MYNAVLIST-pernr   = '00000022'.
P_NODE_RECURSION->BIND_STRUCTURE( NEW_ITEM = P_MYNAVLIST
            SET_INITIAL_ELEMENTS = ABAP_FALSE ).
```

If we want to make the node selectable, we must make sure that the SELECTION_ENABLED property is set as TRUE. Any other appropriate fields must also be set with suitable values for identifying the respective node.

Create the application and activate the necessary service. You can then test the application.

Final Output

Let's assume we are now done with all the steps. Our requirement is to display a list in a hierarchical view – showing the personnel number and name as the top node, and under each top node, the relevant infotypes that are populated. The output of the steps is shown in Figure 11.

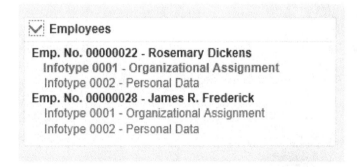

Figure 11: Desired User Output

As mentioned earlier, the layout is defined using the View Editor. The complete code for the WDDOINIT method is shown below:

```
method WDDOINIT .
DATA P_MYNAVLIST TYPE WD_THIS->ELEMENT_NAV_NODE.
DATA P_NODE_NAVI_LIST TYPE REF TO IF_WD_CONTEXT_NODE.
```

```
DATA P_ELEMENT_NAVI_LIST TYPE REF TO IF_WD_CONTEXT_ELEMENT.
DATA P_NODE_RECURSION TYPE REF TO IF_WD_CONTEXT_NODE.

P_NODE_NAVI_LIST = WD_CONTEXT->GET_CHILD_NODE( NAME =
          WD_THIS->WDCTX_NAV_NODE ).

CLEAR P_MYNAVLIST.
P_MYNAVLIST-TEXT    = 'Emp. No. 00000022 - Rosemary Dickens'.
P_MYNAVLIST-SELECT_ENABLED = ABAP_true.
P_MYNAVLIST-infotype  = ''.
P_MYNAVLIST-pernr = '00000022' .

P_ELEMENT_NAVI_LIST  = P_NODE_NAVI_LIST->BIND_STRUCTURE(
          NEW_ITEM      = P_MYNAVLIST
          SET_INITIAL_ELEMENTS = ABAP_FALSE ).

P_NODE_RECURSION =
  P_ELEMENT_NAVI_LIST->GET_CHILD_NODE( NAME = 'NAV_NODE_REC' ).


P_MYNAVLIST-select_enabled = ABAP_TRUE.
P_MYNAVLIST-INFoTYpe    = '0001'.
P_MYNAVLIST-text    = 'Infotype 0001 - Organizational Assignment'.
P_MYNAVLIST-pernr   = '00000022'.
P_NODE_RECURSION->BIND_STRUCTURE( NEW_ITEM = P_MYNAVLIST
          SET_INITIAL_ELEMENTS = ABAP_FALSE ).

P_NODE_RECURSION =
  P_ELEMENT_NAVI_LIST->GET_CHILD_NODE( NAME = 'NAV_NODE_REC' ).

P_MYNAVLIST-select_enabled = ABAP_TRUE.
P_MYNAVLIST-INFoTYpe    = '0001'.
P_MYNAVLIST-text    = 'Infotype 0002 - Personal Data'.
P_MYNAVLIST-pernr   = '00000022'..
P_NODE_RECURSION->BIND_STRUCTURE( NEW_ITEM = P_MYNAVLIST
          SET_INITIAL_ELEMENTS = ABAP_FALSE ).


P_NODE_NAVI_LIST = WD_CONTEXT->GET_CHILD_NODE( NAME =
          WD_THIS->WDCTX_NAV_NODE ).
CLEAR P_MYNAVLIST.
P_MYNAVLIST-TEXT    = 'Emp. No. 00000028 - James R. Frederick'.
P_MYNAVLIST-SELECT_ENABLED = ABAP_true.
P_MYNAVLIST-infotype  = ''.
P_MYNAVLIST-pernr = '28' .

P_ELEMENT_NAVI_LIST  = P_NODE_NAVI_LIST->BIND_STRUCTURE(
          NEW_ITEM      = P_MYNAVLIST
          SET_INITIAL_ELEMENTS = ABAP_FALSE ).
```

```
P_NODE_RECURSION =
  P_ELEMENT_NAVI_LIST->GET_CHILD_NODE( NAME = 'NAV_NODE_REC' ).


P_MYNAVLIST-select_enabled = ABAP_TRUE.
P_MYNAVLIST-INFoTYpe     = '0001'.
P_MYNAVLIST-text     = 'Infotype 0001 - Organizational Assignment'.
P_MYNAVLIST-pernr     = '26'.
 P_NODE_RECURSION->BIND_STRUCTURE( NEW_ITEM = P_MYNAVLIST
             SET_INITIAL_ELEMENTS = ABAP_FALSE ).


P_NODE_RECURSION =
  P_ELEMENT_NAVI_LIST->GET_CHILD_NODE( NAME = 'NAV_NODE_REC' ).

P_MYNAVLIST-select_enabled = ABAP_TRUE.
P_MYNAVLIST-INFoTYpe     = '0002'.
P_MYNAVLIST-text     = 'Infotype 0002 - Personal Data'.
P_MYNAVLIST-pernr     = '26'.
 P_NODE_RECURSION->BIND_STRUCTURE( NEW_ITEM = P_MYNAVLIST
             SET_INITIAL_ELEMENTS = ABAP_FALSE ).


endmethod.
```

Extract the Last N Characters from a String of Any Length Using a Single Line of Code – A Regular Expressions Exercise

I recently came across a simple problem in which I needed to extract the last four characters from a string. For example, if the string had been ACC2344, I would only have needed 2344; had the string been 23ACDD, I would have needed only ACDD. The string in a problem like this could be any length – it could be 4, 10, or even 22 characters long.

So how do we solve this problem?

The answer is to write a simple regular expression and use it with the REPLACE statement, as shown here:

replace first occurrence of regex '(.*) (\S{4})$' in mystring with '$2'.

Let us now review this regular expression.

We have used subgroup registers here. We have created two subgroups. Let me start by explaining the second subgroup, (\S{4}). Here, \S matches any four characters that are non-space characters. In order to make sure that these are at the end of the string, we have used the dollar sign ($), which denotes the end of the string contained in the variable mystring. Now, let's backtrack to the first subgroup. Here, we have used (.*) to denote any set of characters. In other words, this means all the characters within the string that precede the last four.

We have used the REPLACE statement to remove the first subgroup's contents from the string. As a result, after this replacement, only the last four characters remain in string mystring.

Since we are not interested in what comes before the last four characters of the string, we will only specify '$2' as the replacement string and not use the first subgroup's contents (this is why $1 has not been used).

If mystring contains **23ACDD**, its contents after execution of the REPLACE statement will appear as shown in Figure 1.

ACDD
Figure 1: Mystring Contents

Adding Custom Fixed Values to Standard Domains without a Modification Key

We are all aware of fixed values for domains residing in the ABAP Dictionary. A typical requirement we may face while dealing with domains is that we may sometimes need to add custom fixed values to a standard domain. For example, for a status domain with a number of fixed-value texts, we might be required to add a new status that was not originally defined by SAP. It is possible to do this without modifying using the access key. This may be done via the Append Fixed Value function in the data dictionary.

The steps required for this are shown here.

1 Call transaction SE11. Enter the name of the domain you want to enhance in the field provided (in this example, let's use P01_SV_PROCESS_STATUS). It will look as shown in Figure 1.

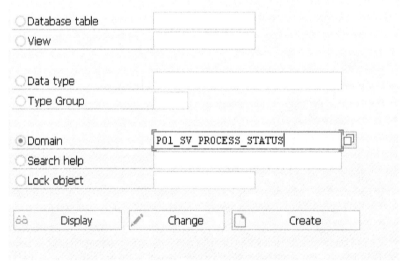

Figure 1: Transaction SE11

2 Click the Display button. Here you will see the existing fixed value range in the standard domain. The screen will appear as shown in Figure 2.

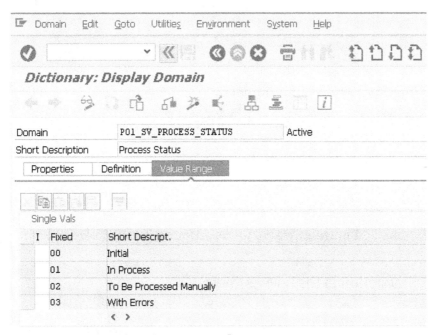

Figure 2: Value Range

As you see, there are several fixed values for the domain. We will now add a new value to this list (this is our requirement).

3 Follow the menu path **Go to → Fixed Value Append**. A dialog box will appear, as shown in Figure 3.

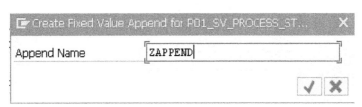

Figure 3: Value Append Dialog

4 Enter the name of the fixed value to be appended in the field provided and click the Continue button. We have given this value the name ZAPPEND. This will take you to the screen shown in Figure 4.

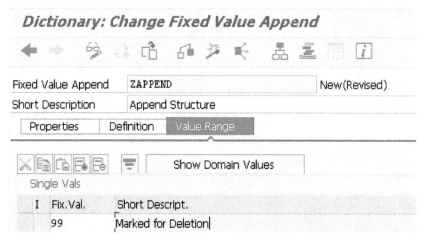

Figure 4: Fixed Value Append ZAPPEND

Enter a short description in the relevant field.

Next, enter the new fixed value code and the short description you would like to add to the existing set of values. In our case, we have added 99 and "Marked for Deletion" as the fixed value and description respectively.

Once this is done, save and activate your domain.

You will now see that the new fixed value has been added to the standard set of values, as shown in Figure 5.

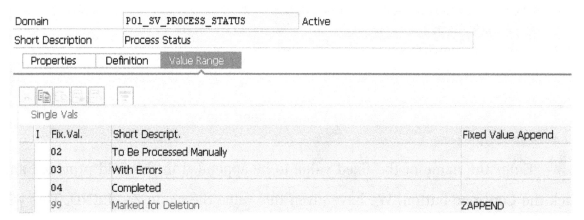

Figure 5: Domain Fixed Values

This set will now be shown in search helps and will also be accessible via domain reading function modules.

For staying up-to-date
with our latest announcements
regarding ERP magazine
issues and books, subscribe to our
ERPMagazine mailing list
at Google Groups

Want high-quality online SAP training?

At the right price?

No long stories, no boring theories.

Want valuable tips and tricks from
the experts to get you project-ready?

We prepare you like no one else does.

For more information about
training in ABAP, Workflow,
Basis, and functional training
across all major modules,
contact us at
training@erpmagazine.net.

ERP Magazine April 2018 – Issue 1

Taking Quick Input from Users with a Standard Function Module

Sometimes, developers must get a value or values from the user and store them in the program for further processing. This requirement can crop up in both dialog programs and reports. SAP's function module POPUP_GETVALUES lets us do this with minimal effort. Here, we will see how to use the function module and learn its main parameters and the corresponding output. This article will answer the following questions:

- What are the most important parameters of the function module?

- What steps are used to call it in ABAP programs?

- What does the module's typical output look like?

Using Function Module POPUP_GETVALUES

Before we dive into the call for the function module POPUP_GETVALUES, let's familiarize ourselves with the key parameters. The function module takes the important parameter FIELDS as input. This parameter is based on the dictionary structure SVAL, which has three important fields: the table name (TABNAME), the field name (FIELDNAME) and the value (VALUE). The table name and field name determine the type and size of the displayed input fields, and the value that the user enters is returned in the VALUE field. Suppose we need to take two fields, employee number, and name, as input from the user via a dialog box.

Let us now look at the steps required, including defining necessary variables, populating them with field names to be displayed on the input dialog and calling the function module.

1 We begin by defining an internal table based on the dictionary structure SVAL and naming it DISPLAYED_FIELDS. We now also define a structure by the name SINGLE_FIELD.

```
data: displayed_fields type table of sval.
data: single_field type sval.
```

2 Next, we add two rows to the internal table. For each input field to be displayed in the input dialog, we need a separate row in the table DISPLAYED_FIELDS. Add two fields, the first for the PERNR (employee number) and the second for the employee name.

```
single_field-tabname = 'PA0003'.
single_field-fieldname = 'PERNR'.
append single_field to displayed_fields.
single_field-tabname  = 'PA0001'.
single_field-fieldname = 'ENAME'.
append single_field to displayed_fields.
```

By default, the sequence of rows here determines the sequence of input fields at runtime. The label of the input field is also taken from the data element text of the table fields.

It is worth noting that you may find the fields you will use as the basis of input in different tables. As you can see, in our case one, the field is from table PA0001, and the other is from PA0003.

3 We now call the function module and then pass the internal table as a parameter.

```
call function 'POPUP_GET_VALUES'
  exporting
   popup_title    = 'Enter Employee Details'
  tables
   fields        = displayed_fields
  exceptions
   error_in_fields = 1
   others       = 2.
```

4 The parameter POPUP_TITLE allows you to define the title of the box. Specify a suitable dialog title to be displayed when the program is executed.

```
read table displayed_fields into single_field
    with key fieldname = 'PERNR'.
if sy-subrc = 0.
 write single_field-value.
endif.
```

The complete code of the program is shown in Code Listing 1.

```
    data: displayed_fields  type table of sval.
    data: single_field  type sval.


    single_field-tabname  = 'PA0003'.
    single_field-fieldname = 'PERNR'.
    append single_field  to displayed_fields.
    single_field-tabname  = PA0001'.
    single_field-fieldname = 'ENAME'.
    append single_field  to displayed_fields.

    call function 'POPUP_GET_VALUES'
     exporting
       popup_title    = 'Enter Employee Details'
     tables
       fields        = displayed_fields
     exceptions
       error_in_fields = 1
       others        = 2.

    read table displayed_fields into single_field
       with key fieldname = 'PERNR'.

    if sy-subrc = 0.
      write single_field-value.
    endif.
    read table displayed_fields into single_field
     with key fieldname = 'ENAME'.
    if sy-subrc = 0.
      write single_field-value.
    endif.
```

When the program is executed, a dialog box appears, as shown in Figure 1. The user may then enter values in the relevant fields. These values are then returned in the VALUE field of the internal table DISPLAYED_FIELDS.

Figure 1: Outputted Dialog Box

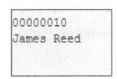

Figure 2: Outputted Data

The output of this is shown in Figure 2.

You can modify this source code to suit your individual requirements.

ALV Row Coloring: A Primer for SAP Developers

Currently, the most familiar data-output format among both users and developers is ABAP List/View ALV. However, developers sometimes come across a tricky requirement: what if the user wants the rows of an ALV output to be color-coded to highlight rows that belong to a particular category or that have vales fulfilling certain criteria?

Many developers are not aware that with some coding and a little extra effort, they can include up to seven colors with different variations and intensities in their ALV outputs. This can help users highlight rows that meet certain criteria.

In this article, we will see how to color rows in ALV output. We will start by considering a few key questions:

- What are the most important steps required in creating an ALV with colors?

- What are the steps required in doing so?

- How many different colors (and shades) may be used in ALV?

Designing an ALV with Colored Rows

We will now look at how to build an ALV report from scratch and add the color-display functionality as we go. Let us assume we are building a sample program that will display the names, numbers, and dates of birth of employees. All employees who are over 60 are to be shown in red, and the others should be shown in yellow. Let us look at the main extra steps required to build this report.

1 First, we define the necessary variables pertaining to the ALV object, functions and columns. We also now define the structure of the table to be outputted.

```
types: begin of ty_emp_birthdates,
        pernr type pa0002-pernr,
        ename type pa0001-ename,
        gbdat type pa0002-gbdat,
        scol  type lvc_t_scol, " Color field"
      end of ty_emp_birthdates.

data: itab_emp type standard table of ty_emp_birthdates,
      wa_emp   type ty_emp_birthdates.
data: myalvtable    type ref to cl_salv_table,
      myalvfunctions type ref to  cl_salv_functions_list,
```

```
myalvcolumns   type ref to cl_salv_columns_table,
myalvcolumn    type ref to cl_salv_column_list.
```

An important part of this step is to specify a field by the name SCOL in the internal table row and corresponding structure. The SCOL component must be based on the LVC_T_SCOL table type defined in the dictionary. This component is actually an internal table which we will populate in the next step.

2 We will then add suitable data to the internal table ITAB_EMP, which will, in turn, add the color information when each row is populated. We also specify the information pertaining to the color, intensity, and inverse of the given rows.

```
"" appending data to ITAB_EMP not shown for simplicity

data wa_color type lvc_s_scol.
sort itab_emp by pernr.
loop at itab_emp assigning field-symbol(<fs_emp>) .
 if <fs_emp>-gbdat lt '19570401'.
  wa_color-color-int  = 1.
  wa_color-color-inv  = 1.
  wa_color-color-col  = 6.
  append wa_color to <fs_emp>-scol.
 else.
  wa_color-color-int  = 0.
  wa_color-color-inv  = 0.
  wa_color-color-col  = 3.
  append wa_color to <fs_emp>-scol.
 endif.
endloop.
```

As you see, we have checked the birthdate GBDAT of the employee. If the employee is over 60, i.e., the date of birth is before 1 April 1957, the COL column of the table is assigned color 6, red.

Table 1 shows the colors available for ALV tables and the relevant code for each color.

Color Code	Color
1	Gray-blue
2	Light gray
3	Yellow
4	Blue-green
5	Green
6	Red
7	Violet

Table 1: Possible ALV Color Codes

Here, we have assigned a value of 6 to the color for the row when the employee is older than 60. Yellow (value 3) is specified for rows where the employee is under 60 years of age.

For red rows, the intensified (INT) and inverse (INV) properties are switched on (i.e., 1). For yellow rows, these two properties are switched off.

Note: It is essential that the SET_COLOR_COLUMN method is called before the ALV DISPLAY method.

1 We then call the FACTORY method of the CL_SALV_TABLE class. The most important thing here is that the SET_COLOR_COLUMN method of the CL_SALV_COLUMNS_TABLE is called for the object mycolumns. This specifies which column in the ALV contains the information the colors pertain to. The code of this step is shown below:

```
cl_salv_table=>factory(      importing
    r_salv_table = myalvtable      changing
    t_table    = itab_emp ).


    ........
  myalvcolumns->set_color_column( value = 'SCOL' ).

  myalvtable->display( ).
```

The output of the program is shown in Figure 1.

ALV Row Coloring Example

Emp. Number	Empl./appl.name	Date of Birth
10	James Reed	11.08.1982
128	John Adams	17.10.1942
425	Stephanie Pabon	20.02.1978
825	Rosalyn Adams	19.04.1976
7510	Michelle James	07.01.1947
8510	Krista Mitchell	14.01.1941

Figure 1: Program Output

The complete code for this requirement is shown here:

```
start-of-selection.
  "" appending data to ITAB_EMP not shown for simplicity
sort itab_emp by pernr.
loop at itab_emp assigning field-symbol(<fs_emp>) .
  if <fs_emp>-gbdat lt '19570401'.
    wa_color-color-int  = 1.
    wa_color-color-inv  = 1.
    wa_color-color-col  = 6.
    append wa_color to <fs_emp>-scol.
  else.
    wa_color-color-int  = 0.
    wa_color-color-inv  = 0.
   wa_color-color-col  = 3.
    append wa_color to <fs_emp>-scol.
  endif.
endloop.

  try. cl_salv_table=>factory(
     importing
       r_salv_table = myalvtable
     changing
       t_table     = itab_emp ).

  myalvfunctions = myalvtable->get_functions( ).
  myalvfunctions->set_all( abap_true ).

  myalvcolumns = myalvtable->get_columns( ).
  myalvcolumn ?= myalvcolumns->get_column( 'PERNR' ).
```

```
      myalvcolumn->set_long_text( 'Emp. Number' ).
      myalvcolumn ?= myalvcolumns->get_column( 'ENAME' ).
      myalvcolumn->set_long_text( 'Employee Name' ).
      myalvcolumn ?= myalvcolumns->get_column( 'GBDAT' ).
      myalvcolumn->set_long_text( 'Date of Birth' ).

      myalvcolumns->set_color_column( value = 'SCOL' ).

    myalvtable->display( ).
    catch cx_salv_msg.
    catch cx_salv_data_error.
    catch cx_salv_not_found.
endtry.
```

A Simple Regular Expression Exercise

Regular expressions (regex) allow you to carry out validation and to replace text and text patterns quickly and easily. The major advantage of regex is that it fulfills the requirements of a long block of code in a single line or a few lines of code. To demonstrate, consider a simple requirement:

You have a string that ends with a comma sign (,). It consists of a number of values separated by commas, and the string also ends with a comma. Your task is to remove the last comma from the string.
The string could be of any length, and you are not sure of the positions of the commas within the string.
For example:

> JonREED, Sam, Houston,
>
> Samuel, Tom, Boston,

One approach to this problem is to first calculate the length of the string and then subtract one from it and remove the comma at that point.

The code for this is shown in here:

```
// bad approach
    len = strlen( mystring ).
    index = len - 1.
        IF   mystring+index(1) = '|'.
            mystring = mystring+0(index).
        ENDIF.
```

In this case, we cannot use a SPLIT statement as we may have a number of commas within the text, only the last of which has to be removed.

A better and more compact approach is to use regular expressions. In this case, we will use the regular expression **(.*)\,\$** to solve our problem.

We will see how the above requirement may be solved using a REPLACE statement in conjunction with a suitable regular expression. Though there may be multiple regexes for this requirement, we will only look at one regex that will solve our problem here.

The regex has two parts:
> (.*): This part matches any number of characters in the string (excluding the last character). Since we need this part, round brackets have been used.

\,$: This is the main part of the regex. We want to match the comma at the end of the string; hence the dollar sign. Putting this into brackets will not make any difference, as we are only interested in the first part of the regular expression.

We use .* to find any number of characters in the string (except the last one). We enclose this in parentheses, which help us create subgroup registers. Since we need to match a special character (in our case, a comma) within the regex, we use a backslash. So, attempts to find a comma; since $ means the end of the string, with the $ sign included, it finds the last comma in the string.

Using this regular expression, any number of fields separated by commas may be corrected and extracted (after removal of the last comma).

The statement REPLACE is used in this case, as shown here:

REPLACE FIRST OCCURRENCE OF REGEX '(.*)\,$' IN my string WITH '$1'.

It is essential to write REGEX in this statement; otherwise, the statement will not function.

The dollar sign with the number one ($1) is used as the replacement string. The placeholder $1 represents the contents of the first subgroup register. This, in fact, will contain the entire string except for the last comma. For a string ending with a comma, the executed program returns the string with the last comma removed. For example, suppose the content of MYSTRING is:

James, And, Qrange,

After execution of the REPLACE statement, the content of MYSTRING will be:

James, And,Orange

Since we do not need the last comma, we do not store it in a subgroup register (hence, we have not used parentheses). The $1 in the replacement string denotes that the replacement will include the entire set of characters except for the last comma. Thus, our requirements are fulfilled.

If the string MYSTRING does not finish with a comma, the string is returned as it was before the statement.

Note that you may use REPLACE ALL OCCURRENCES as well since we are looking for a single character that occurs only once (the final comma). Because of this, both

REPLACE the FIRST OCCURRENCE and REPLACE ALL OCCURRENCES will have the same effect. Moreover, if you have a number of rows in a given table, you can use the single statement REPLACE ... TABLE variant. There is no need to explicitly loop on the given internal table and carry out regular expression processing.

Using Debugger Standard Functions for Skipping as well as moving Back within Code

Within the ABAP debugger, developers are familiar with common functions such as Single Step via F5 or skipping through a method or form routine using the F6 key. Within the Debugger, it is also possible to skip execution of certain lines of code or to go back to a particular line that has already been executed and execute it again. This presents a clear advantage as a time-saver when we are debugging a very large program, and we want to go back to a certain line without having to start debugging all over again.

To make things clear, consider a simple example. Suppose we have a program that is being debugged, as shown in Figure 1. For whatever reason, we have reached line 16 and missed program behavior in the previous lines.

```
 8    data a   type i  .
 9
10    a = 0.
11
12    write : / a.
13
14    a = a + 1.
15
16    write a.
```

Figure 1: Example Program

Say we want to go back to line 12. We can do this by simply placing the cursor at line 12 and then using the menu option Debugger → Goto Statement (see Figure 2), or we can use the keys Shift + F12.

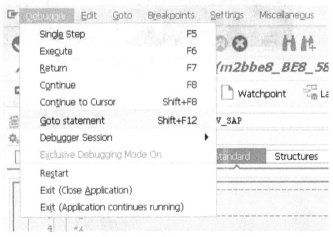

Figure 2: Debugger Menu

This will take the program execution back to line 12. One important thing here to keep in mind is that bringing the execution pointer back to a line that was already executed earlier will not undo any change (in the state of the variable) that the line had produced. If the variable has been incremented (as in our case) then going back will not affect the value of variable A (i.e., will not set that as 0) to which it was when the first time line 12 was executed. (See Figure 3.)

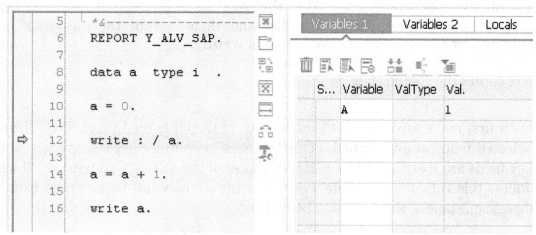

Figure 3: Insert Caption

It is also possible to skip a particular block of code using the **Go to Statement** menu option. Suppose our cursor is now at line 12 of the code, but we want to skip execution of lines 13 to 15 and to have the execution arrow go directly to line 16. To do this, we simply place the cursor at the line immediately after the block we want to skip (in our case, this will be line 16). Once this is done, we use Go to Statement again. This will bring the execution pointer to the intended line of code.

Suppose at line 12, the value of A is 1, and the execution of line 14 is skipped. This will mean that the value of A will not be incremented. It will remain as 1, i.e., the value it had at line 12. (If the line were not skipped, the value of A would be 2.)

A Little-Known Problem of the "FOR ALL ENTRIES IN" Construct

We often hear about the things to keep in mind with the FOR ALL ENTRIES IN(FAEI) variant of SELECT; let's walk through it in more depth. Let's pull back the curtain on a simple problem related to the behavior of this variant of the SELECT statement. We will look at an example, and then explain the output of such statements that **seems correct** but in fact **is wrong**.

So here comes the golden rule:

We must first make sure that all the keys fields of the table read via an FAEI listed in the selected field list are fetched. (This becomes even more necessary when not all the key fields are specified in the WHERE clause of the SELECT statement.) If we do not follow this rule, the complete, correct result set may not be returned from the database, i.e., some of the rows may be omitted.

Let us understand this rule via a simple piece of code. This program compiles successfully and gives no message when running in a code inspector or extended code check.

```
types : begin of my_type,
        lgart type t512t-lgart,
        lgtxt type t512t-lgtxt,
        end of my_type.

data : it_driver type standard table of molga.
data : it_data type standard table of my_type.
append '01' to it_driver.

select lgart lgtxt
  from t512t into corresponding fields of table it_data
  for all entries in it_driver  where molga eq it_driver-table_line.

write : 'Total Records Fetched ', sy-dbcnt.
```

In this code fragment, we are reading the fields LGART and LGTXT from the table T512T via the FAEI variant. We have not included the key fields MOLGA and SPRSL of the database table T512T from the selection field list. The internal table IT_DRIVER has a single row including 01, which is then used in the WHERE clause condition corresponding to MOLGA. The result set of this code omits a number of entries that should have been read. This result will then have an incorrect value, in our example 8,785, as shown in Figure 4.

```
Total Records Fetched     8,785
```

Figure 4: Wrong Value Displayed

Let us see how we can correct the code:

```
types : begin of my_type,
       sprsl type t512t-sprsl,
       molga type t512t-molga,1
       lgart type t512t-lgart,
       lgtxt type t512t-lgtxt,
       end of my_type.

data : it_driver type standard table of molga.
data : it_data type standard table of my_type.
append '01' to it_driver.

select sprsl molga lgart lgtxt
  from t512t into corresponding fields of table it_data
  for all entries in it_driver
  where molga eq it_driver-table_line.

write : 'Total Records Fetched ', sy-dbcnt.
```

We have changed the coding slightly. As you see, we have added two more fields MOLGA and SPRSL to the type MY_TYPE. Likewise, in the SELECT field list, the fields MOLGA and SPRSL are also included. When this code is executed, the correct number of database records are returned in the table IT_DATA. The output of the system now shows 8,188, the correct figure (we can check this against the Number of Entries feature of the transaction SE11). This is shown in Figure 5.

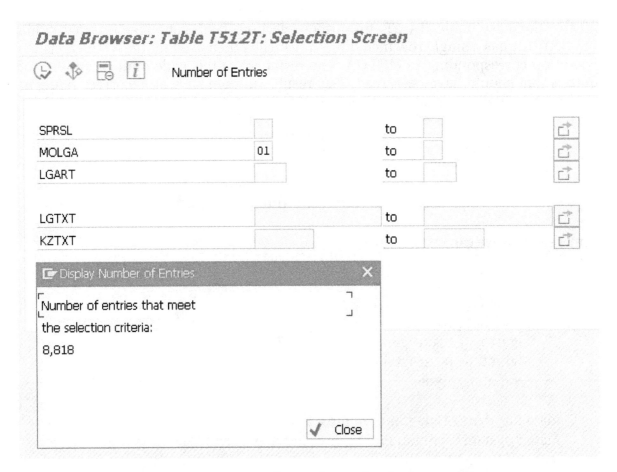

Figure 5: Number of Entries in T512T

Specifying Exporting and Returning Parameters for Functional Methods

Most developers think that functional methods only return a value computed within the method and that they cannot have exporting parameters. Since the newer NetWeaver releases, it has been possible for methods to have both returning and exporting parameters. This means we can create both locally and globally functional methods with exporting and importing parameters as well as returning ones. Such functional methods may be static or may be instance methods.

In this article, we will see how to define such methods both locally and globally. For simplicity, we will create a static method to fulfill our requirement.

Consider that we have a static method AVERAGE_AND_TOTAL that calculates both the average and the total of two numbers. We can set the average as the returning parameter and the total as the exporting parameter. The class will then look like this:

```
class myclass definition.
  public section.
    types :  ty_dec2 type p length 13 decimals 2.
    class-methods  average_and_total  importing
                      int1 type i
                      int2 type i
                   exporting
                      total type i
                   returning
                      value(average) type ty_ dec2.
  endclass.
```

We have defined a type TY_DEC2 within the class on which the AVERAGE parameter is based.
As you see, we have defined a class locally within the program. This class has a static method by the name AVERAGE, and this method has two numbers by the name INTEGERS. The AVERAGE is specified as a returning parameter and the TOTAL as an exporting parameter for the method in question.

The implementation of the class will have the detailed method code. Here we will calculate the average and the total of the two numbers supplied:

```
class myclass implementation.
  method average_and_total.
    total = int1 + int2.
    average = total / 2.
  endmethod.
endclass.
```

We can call this method a number of ways. For example, using the assignment operator, it is possible to use this method to read only the average value of the two numbers. This is shown in the code below:

```
start-of-selection.
  data(average) = myclass=>average_and_total( int1 = 4 int2 = 10 ) .
  write : average , 'is the average '.
```

This returns the average of the two numbers, which is then printed on the screen. We use inline declaration for the variable AVERAGE. Note here that we have not specified and imported the parameter TOTAL.

It is also possible to call the static method AVERAGE_AND_TOTAL and import the total using the TOTAL parameter, as well as to use the retuned AVERAGE value in an expression using the assignment operator. An example of this is shown here:

```
new-line.
data total type i.
data(average2) = myclass=>average_and_total(
                  exporting
                    int1 = 8
                    int2 = 2
                  importing
                    total = total ) .
write : average2 , 'is the average and the total is ',
        total LEFT-JUSTIFIED.
```

Here, we pass the values 8 and 2 for INT1 and INT2 respectively. The value of the average is returned in variable AVERAGE2, and the total is assigned to variable TOTAL. The output is then printed on the screen, as shown in Figure 6.

```
7.00  is the average
5.00  is the average and the total is  10
```

Figure 6: Caption

A similar method may be defined globally using the Class Builder transaction SE24. The method definition tab will look as shown in Figure 7.

Class/Interface	ZCL_MY_CLASS			Implemented / Active	

Properties	Interfaces	Friends	Attributes	Methods	Events	Types

Parameters of Method   AVERAGE_AND_TOTAL

← Methods	⚡	Exceptions	📋 Sourcecode	📇 Properties	📑 📑

Parameter	Type	Pass Value	Optional	Typing Method	Associated Type
INT1	Importing	☐	☐	Type	I
INT2	Importing	☐	☐	Type	I
TOTAL	Exporting	☐	☐	Type	I
AVERAGE	Returning	✓	☐	Type	TY_DEC2
		☐	☐	Type	
		☐	☐	Type	

Figure 7: Method Definition

As you see, the TOTAL parameter is specified as an exporting parameter, whereas AVERAGE is defined as a returning parameter. The type TY_DEC2 is defined on the TYPES tab. The output of the method from the SE24 transaction test screen is shown in Figure 8.

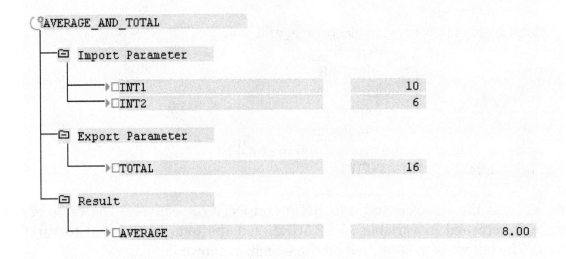

Figure 8: Testing Method AVERAGE_AND_TOTAL

Debugging Applications after Modal Dialog Displayed

You may come across situations in which you must start the Debugger after the display of a modal dialog box. Under normal circumstances, you need to close the modal dialog box, as you are not allowed to put /h in the command field or start a new session and insert a break point. In this short article, we will discuss a technique that enables us to start the debugger and reach the correct location in the program code after the modal dialog display.
Here are some of the steps required to start the debugger.

We first need to create a text file in Notepad with the following text:

```
[FUNCTION]
Command=/H
Title=Debugger
Type=SystemCommand
```

Save this file with the name debugger.txt on the Desktop.

Make sure that the text shown is correctly written in the text file.

Once this is done, start the program that will display the dialog box. When this dialog box appears, drag and drop the Debugger.txt file onto the title bar of the dialog box. This will start the debugger, as shown in Figure 1.

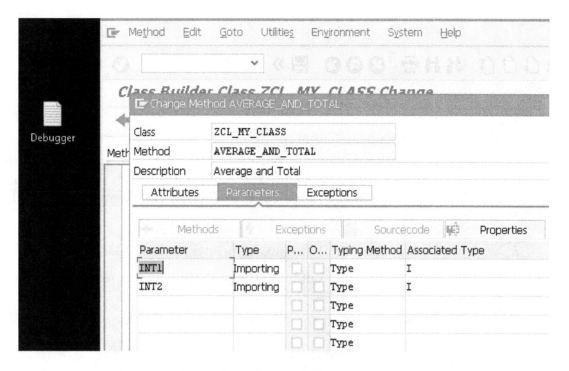

Figure 1: Starting the Debugger

This will display the message shown in Figure 2.

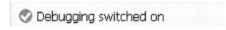

Figure 2: Debugger Switched on

This takes you to the desired location in the application program, as shown in Figure 3.

```
 1
 2    process before output.
 3
 4      module status_0210.
 5      call subscreen sss including 'SAPLSEOD
 6
 7    process after input.
 8
 9      module exit_dynpro_0210 at exit-comman
10      module manage_ok_code_0210.
11      call subscreen sss.
12      module user_commmand_0210.
```

Figure 3: Debugging Location

Four Easy Coding Steps to Execute a Program in Background

We are all aware of the SUBMIT statement. It is used to call another program via a selection screen, and display the output of the called program on the user screen. It is however also possible to execute the called program in the background using a SUBMIT statement. This requires some additional function module calls such as JOB_OPEN and JOB_CLOSE. Let us see how this is done:

1 The first step here is to declare appropriate variables that will be used for supplying the necessary parameters to the respective function modules.

```
DATA: number TYPE tbtcjob-jobcount,
    name   TYPE tbtcjob-jobname VALUE 'JOBCALLTEST',
    print_parameters TYPE pri_params.
...
```

1   Within the main program, we call the function module JOB_OPEN to open a new job. We specify Jobname as a parameter.

```
CALL FUNCTION 'JOB_OPEN'
  EXPORTING
    jobname      = name
  IMPORTING
    jobcount      = number
  EXCEPTIONS
    cant_create_job = 1
    invalid_job_data = 2
    jobname_missing  = 3
    OTHERS       = 4.
```

2   Once this is done and the call to the function module JOB_OPEN is successful, we call the SUBMIT statement along with the SAP-SPOOL variant. In this step, we also specify the job number and use **RETURN**. We pass the print parameters and use the WITHOUT SPOOL DYNPRO addition in order to make sure that no Print dialog is displayed.

```
SUBMIT ZCALLED_PROGRAM TO SAP-SPOOL
       SPOOL PARAMETERS print_parameters
       WITHOUT SPOOL DYNPRO
       VIA JOB name NUMBER number
       AND RETURN.
```

If there are any parameters on the screen of the program, they may be passed via the SELECTION -SCREEN addition.

3 Here, we need to make sure that the job is closed so that we will call the function module JOB_ CLOSE.

```
CALL FUNCTION 'JOB_CLOSE'
   EXPORTING
      jobcount      = number
      jobname       = name
      strtimmed     = 'X'
   EXCEPTIONS
      cant_start_immediate = 1
      invalid_startdate   = 2
      jobname_missing     = 3
      job_close_failed    = 4
      job_nosteps     = 5
      job_notex       = 6
      lock_failed     = 7
      OTHERS          = 8.
```

The job number and the job name are passed to parameters JOBCOUNT and JOBNAME respectively. Moreover, the STRTIMMED (start immediately) parameter is passed a value of 'X' so that the program execution may be immediately started. Once the code is executed, the called program is run in the background. Any output from the called program is not displayed on the screen. Moreover, any changes or updates specified in the called program are committed to the database.

Learn to Determine Employee Locking Programmatically

Whion programming an HCM application, developers may come across scenarios in which they are required to check whether personnel or employee number is locked or not. Based on this, certain processing maybe is done, or a certain block of code be executed. One way of doing this is via the function module ENQUEUE_READ.

This article aims to show how to use the function module to determine whether an employee is locked for processing or not, and the various parameters passed in order to get the desired result. The function module essentially searches for locked entries in the transaction SM12, as this may contain entries pertaining to locked employees. The SM12 entry for locked personnel numbers is shown in Figure 1.

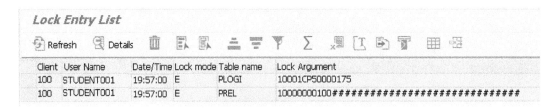

Figure 1: Transaction SM12

The function module ENQUEUE_READ has a number of parameters. These are:

- GCLIENT. This is the three-digit client number specifying which client's lock status is to be checked.

- GNAME. This is the name of the lock object relevant to the scenario. This may either be a standard lock object or a custom one. To check personnel number, we use the PREL lock object. This is the table name value shown in Figure 1.

- GARG. This is the most important parameter and denotes the lock argument pertaining to the key vales that we need to determine.

- GUNAME. This parameter specifies the user name that has locked the employee. If you do not want to specify this, pass * as the user name. This will tell you if the given employee has been locked by any user ID.

Now that we have a basic idea of the function module and its parameters let us look at some basic coding:

```
Data lock_argument type string .

    concatenate sy-mandt mypernr '*' into lock_argument .
    call function 'ENQUEUE_READ'
      exporting
        gclient          = sy-mandt
        gname            = 'PREL'
        garg             = lock_argument
        guname           = '*'
      importing
        number           = number
      tables
        enq              = enq
      exceptions
        communication_failure = 1
        system_failure       = 2
        others               = 3.
```

We first assign to the lock argument the value concatenate by the client (sy-mandt), followed by the employee number (mypernr) and ending with an asterisk *. In our case, the lock object is PREL. We have used the asterisk * for the user name since we want to determine whether the employee lock entries have been imposed by any user ID.

The NUMBER returns the number of lock entries found in the transaction SM12 that correspond to the arguments passed. If this value is greater than 0, this means that at least one employee has been locked by another user. Appropriate checks and messages relevant to our requirement may then be added to the program:

```
if sy-subrc eq 0 and number gt 0.
  message 'Employee Already Locked' type 'I'.
  exit.
endif.
```

Learn to Find Whether a Payroll Area Is Locked for Maintenance

W hile programming HR applications, it may be necessary to determine whether a given payroll area is locked for maintenance. (This happens when the payroll of a given period is released.) Based on this, certain processing or validations may be required. ABAP developers may use the class CL_HR_ PAYROLL_AREA for this purpose.

In this short article, we will see how to use the methods and attributes of this class to check the status of a given payroll area. Before going into the details, it is a good idea to familiarize yourself with the attributes and methods of the class CL_HR_PAYROLL_AREA. The methods tab is shown in Figure 1.

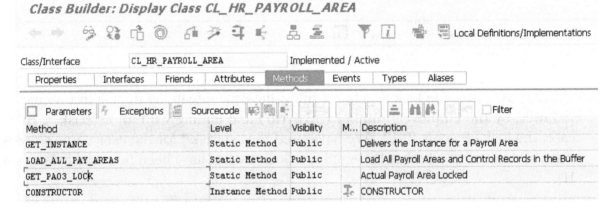

Figure 1: Methods Tab

This class has a method GET_INSTANCE that will return a reference to an instantiated object of the class. The parameters of the method are shown in Figure 2.

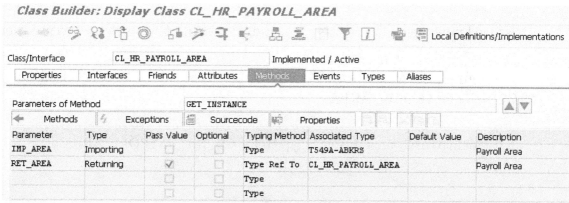

Figure 2: Method Parameters

The class has a number of attributes, some of which are shown in Figure 3.

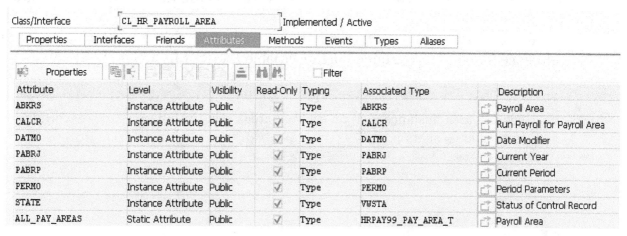

Figure 3: CL_HR_PAYROLL_AREA Attributes

CL_HR_PAYROLL_AREA has an important attribute STATE that tells us the current state of the payroll area control record. This lets us determine whether the payroll area is locked for maintenance or not. The various values that the attribute may have been shown in Table 1.

State	Meaning
0	New
1	Released for payroll
2	Payroll correction
3	Exit payroll
4	Check payroll results
9	Deleted

Table 1: State Values

Now that we know the basics of this class and its method let us see how to use them.

1 We define a reference variable PAYROLL_AREA_INSTANCE based on class CL_HR_PAYROLL_ AREA.

```
data payroll_area_instance type ref to CL_HR_PAYROLL_AREA.
```

2 We pass the payroll area, for example 'A1,' via the variable ABKRS to the static method GET_
INSTANCE. These will instantiate the payroll area object pertaining to A1, the reference for which is contained in the variable PAYROLL_AREA_INSTANCE.

```
payroll_area_instance = cl_hr_payroll_area=>get_instance(          exporting
imp_abkrs = abkrs ) .
```

3 We now check the attribute STATE. If the value of this attribute is equal to 1, the payroll area is locked. A value of zero or anything other than 1means that it is not locked.

```
case payroll_area_instance->state.
    When '1'.
        Write 'Payroll area locked for Maintenance'.
    When others.
        Write 'Not locked'.
endcase.
```

For staying up-to-date
with our latest announcements
regarding ERP magazine
issues and books, subscribe to our
ERPMagazine mailing list
at Google Groups

How to Read Fixed Values of a Domain in Your Programs

When creating ABAP programs, you may come across situations in which you need to use the fixed value and description stored in the dictionary domains. Suppose a value has the code '01' stored in it, but the user wants to see the description (e.g., Description 1) in the program rather than the code. In such cases, one option is to use a CASE...ENDCASE control structure to specify the field values (typically codes) and their appropriate descriptions. However, this is not an elegant approach, and it may make the program verbose when there are a large number of descriptions at the domain level. Also, any additional values updated into the custom domain will not apply to the program automatically and will require code adjustments.

A more useful approach is to choose the standard function module DDUT_DOMVALUES_GET. The values read from the dictionary are returned in an internal table, which may then be processed further within the program. The function module may be used to read domain fixed values for both standard and custom-defined domains. In this article, we will see how this is programmatically done.

Note: Although the primary emphasis of this article is on reading fixed single values for a domain, it is also possible to read the applicable domain value ranges into the program.

Suppose we have a domain ZST6_MY_DOMAIN that has single values ranging from 01 to 04.Partial values are shown in Figure 1.

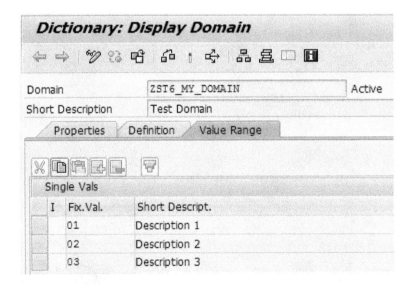

Figure 1: Domain Fixed Values

For each domain value, a description has been specified. Instead of hard coding each value and its description in a CASE ...ENDCASE control structure, we will use the function module DDUT_DOMVALUES_ GET in our program. Let's see how this is done.

We first declare an internal table based on the data dictionary view DD07V. We pass this as a TABLES parameter to the function module, which we then call. For the parameter NAME, we specify the domain to be read from the database (in our case, ZST6_MY_DOMAIN). By default, we choose to take the texts in the system language (hence, we pass SY-LANGU for parameter LANGU).

```
data value_tab type STANDARD TABLE OF DD07V.
call function
'DDUT_DOMVALUES_GET'
    exporting
        name        = 'ZST6_MY_DOMAIN'
        langu       = sy-langu
        texts_only  = 'X'        tables
        dd07v_tab   = value_tab
    exceptions
        ILLEGAL_INPUT = 1
        others        = 0.
```

Once the function module is called and is successful, the table VALUE_TAB is populated as displayed in Figure 2 (shown in the debugger).

	Tables	Table Contents		

Table	VALUE_TAB		
Attributes	Standard [4x9(272)]		
Insert Column		Columns ...	

Row	DOMNAME [C(30)]	VALPOS [N(4)]	DOMVALUE_L [C(10)]	DDTEXT [C(60)]
1	ZST6_MY_DOMAIN	0001	01	Description 1
2	ZST6_MY_DOMAIN	0002	02	Description 2
3	ZST6_MY_DOMAIN	0003	03	Description 3
4	ZST6_MY_DOMAIN	0004	04	Description 4

Figure 2: Values Read from the Domain

These values may then be used for further processing in the program.

Distinctions between the Two Behaviors of the SUBMIT Statement

SUBMIT is a common statement known to ABAP developers. Briefly put, it is used for calling one program from another program. In this article, we will discuss the following two variants of the SUBMIT statement:

- SUBMIT... VIA SELECTION-SCREEN

- SUBMIT... USING SELECTION-SCREEN

These two look quite similar, and a developer could easily assume there is little distinction between them. However, there is a noticeable difference in output when they are executed.

The form SUBMITS...VIA SELECTION-SCREEN takes you to the selection screen of the called program. The user may then enter data into the selection screen and execute the program in order to display the output. In this case, the report output is **not** automatically shown.

On the other hand, the form SUBMITS....USING SELECTION-SCREEN takes you to the output of the called program. The user does not need to enter any data on the selection screen or execute the program to manually display the output. The SUBMIT statement automatically takes you to the output of the called program.

Before we look at code samples, let us assume that we have a program containing the code shown below.

```
PARAMETERS : string TYPE c LENGTH 10 DEFAULT 'Output'.

START-OF-SELECTION.
 WRITE string.
```

This program simply prints the value entered for the parameter STRING (on the selection screen) when F8 is pressed. Remember, F8 is pressed when the selection screen appears, and any value is entered.

We can then use one of the two forms of the SUBMIT statement. The code below uses SUBMIT...VIA SELECTION-SCREEN.

```
SUBMIT zst6_called_program
    VIA SELECTION-SCREEN
    WITH string = 'EXP_STRING'.
```

For the input field STRING, the value EXP_STRING is supplied via the SUBMIT statement. When the program is executed, the selection screen of the called program appears, as shown in Figure 1.

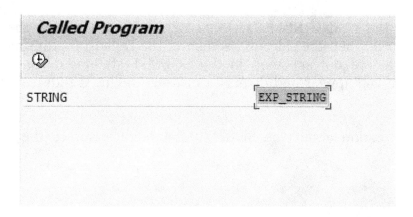

Figure 1: Program Selection Screen

The **output** of the program is not shown. We use this form when we want the user to see the selection screen of the called program and **not** the output directly.

Now let's look at the second variant. A simple code that calls the same program is shown.

```
SUBMIT zst6_program_to_be_called
    USING SELECTION-SCREEN 1000
    WITH string = 'EXP_STRING'.
```

As you can see, we have used USING SELECTION-SCREEN followed by the screen number (for our example report ZST6_PROGRAM_TO_BE_CALLED, it is 1000). The STRING input field is used the same way as in the form shown earlier. The output of this program is shown in Figure 5.

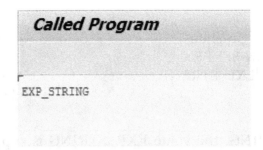

Figure 2: Output of Called Program

The only time the USING SELECTION-SCREEN form will stop the user at the selection screen is when the selection screen of the called program has mandatory input fields that are not specified in the SUBMIT statement. In that case, the selection screen will appear and display a message saying a required field input is missing.

For more information about the SUBMIT statement, refer to the standard SAP documentation.

Use the Two Variants of the CALL TRANSACTION Statement with Ease

Many developers are aware of the CALL TRANSACTION statement. Did you know that it is possible to call a given transaction (from a program) and bypass any authorization checks for the current user executing the main program? As of recent releases, we have the option to call the transaction with or without an authority check. In this article, we will discuss the two variants of the CALL TRANSACTION statement.

The two variants of the CALL TRANSACTION statement are:

... WITH AUTHORITY-CHECK
... WITHOUT AUTHORITY-CHECK

> Note: One of the additions WITH or WITHOUT AUTHORITY-CHECK must be used. Using CALL TRANSACTION without either variant is obsolete and must not be used.

Let us now see these in detail:

... WITH AUTHORITY-CHECK

Using the WITH AUTHORITY-CHECK variant, the current user authorizations to run the relevant transaction – using the S_TCODE authorization object and any authority object specified in SE93 – are checked. If authorization is not found, an exception based on the class CX_SY_AUTHORIZATION_ ERROR is generated.

A simple block of code that uses this form of transaction call would be:

```
TRY .
 CALL TRANSACTION 'AL01' WITH AUTHORITY-CHECK.
CATCH CX_SY_AUTHORIZATION_ERROR.
 WRITE 'NO AUTHORIZATION'.
ENDTRY.
```

Here, we have called the transaction Al01 with authorization check. If the user has the necessary authorization, the transaction is called. Otherwise, the exception CX_SY_AUTHORIZATION_ERROR is raised, which is caught in our program.

When the user does not have authorization, the appropriate message is printed on the screen.

This is the best way to check authorization for the current user and replaces the authority check statement and function module AUTHORITY_CHECK_TCODE.

... WITHOUT AUTHORITY-CHECK

The addition WITHOUT AUTHORITY-CHECK does just the opposite. It does not check any of the authorizations for the current user. An example of this would be:

```
CALL TRANSACTION 'AL01' WITHOUT AUTHORITY-CHECK.
```

Here, the statement bypasses any authorization check. Any user can call the transaction, regardless of authorization.

For staying up-to-date
with our latest announcements
regarding ERP magazine
issues and books, subscribe to our

ERPMagazine mailing list

at Google Groups

Setting Default Ranges for Selection Options upon Declaration

Most developers know about selection options (or select options), which allow us to input a range of values via the selection screen. To set default values or ranges for a given select option, developers commonly uses the ABAP statement APPEND to add rows to the selection option internal table. This is typically done in the INITIALIZATION event. It is, however, also possible to assign a single value or a single range of values directly while defining the select option.

In this article, we will see how to do this, and the various errors that may occur due to wrongly combining the input range's sign and option.

Before diving into the details, let us look at the syntax of a SELECT-OPTIONS statement:

```
SELECT-OPTIONS seloptions FOR table_field
[DEFAULT range_start [TO range_end] [OPTION myoption] [SIGN mysign]]
```

Here we have the declaration, based on a given table or structure field. We first specify the name of the field on which the SELECT-OPTIONS statement is based, followed by the values of the low and high ends of the range, and then the option and the sign. (we must specify the option, such as EQ, BT and the sign (I or E)).
Now let us look at a few examples of this, starting with a simple form. For example, we can specify a single value via the code:

```
tables t512t.
select-options mysel for t512t-lgart DEFAULT '0100'.
```

Here we have a selection option MYSEL based on LGART where the value 0100 for wage type will be set as default. The selection screen resulting from this code is shown in Figure 1.

| Wage Type | 0100 | to | |

Figure 1: Default Single Value

We can also write code specifying a range to be included as a selection criterion. We can, for example, specify the range from 0100 to 0200 wage types by using the following code:

```
select-options mysel2 for t512t-lgart DEFAULT '0100' TO '0200' OPTION BT
SIGN I.
```

As you see, we have specified a range using the DEFAULT ...TO variant of the SELECT-OPTIONS statement. Here, the option is specified as BT, and the SIGN is set as I. The selection screen, in this case, will look like the one shown in Figure 2.

Figure 2: Specifying Ranges

Let us now consider another example:

```
select-options mysel3 for t512t-lgart DEFAULT '0100' TO '0200' OPTION BT
SIGN E.
```

Here, we have specified the same range as earlier, but we have made sure that this range is not included in the selection. We have done this by specifying sign E – i.e., exclude – instead of I. Once the program is executed, the selection screen appears as shown in Figure 3.

Figure 3: Excluding Ranges

We must be careful when using the options and the sign addition to SELECT-OPTIONS. Syntax errors may appear when we use the options wrongly. For example, using Option EQ along with ranges may result in a syntax error, as shown in Figure 4.

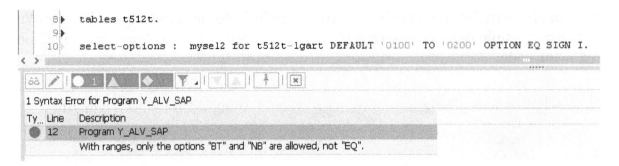

```
  8  tables t512t.

  9

 10  select-options :  mysel2 for t512t-lgart DEFAULT '0100' TO '0200' OPTION EQ SIGN I.
```

1 Syntax Error for Program Y_ALV_SAP

Ty...	Line	Description
●	12	Program Y_ALV_SAP
		With ranges, only the options "BT" and "NB" are allowed, not "EQ".

Figure 4: Syntax Error

Here we have used a range but used EQ instead of BT (between) or NB (not between). For wrongly used combinations, the program will not compile and will produce syntax errors.

Learn How to Determine if a Posting Date lies in an Open or Closed Period

Programmers developing in the FI module may sometimes need to determine whether a given posting date falls in a closed or an open period. A combination of several standard function modules may be used to do this. We will see, in this article, how to use these function modules to solve our requirement.

The steps needed to use these function modules are:

1 We start by finding the period corresponding to the given posting date. We assume here that the posting date BUDAT is contained in the variable MYDATE. We must know the BUKRS – i.e., the company code – as well. We need to find the period POPER and the year corresponding to the given date. For example, the date 01.01.2018 may be in the period 01/2018 (i.e., GJAHR – 2018 and POPER – 01), and so on. To find the period and the year, we call the function module FI_PERIOD_DETERMINE:

```
DATA GJAHR TYPE BKPF-GJAHR.
DATA POPER TYPE T009B-POPER.
CLEAR POPER. CLEAR GJAHR.

CALL FUNCTION 'FI_PERIOD_DETERMINE'
  EXPORTING
    I_BUDAT     = MYDATE
    I_BUKRS     = MYBUKRS
  IMPORTING
    E_GJAHR     = MYGJAHR
    E_POPER     = MYPOPER
  EXCEPTION
    FISCAL_YEAR   = 1
    PERIOD        = 2
    PERIOD_VERSION = 3
    POSTING_PERIOD = 4
    SPECIAL_PERIOD = 5
    VERSION       = 6
    POSTING_DATE  = 7
    OTHERS        = 8.
```

Once the function module is successfully executed, the year and the period are contained in the variables MYGJAHR and MYPOPER respectively. These will be used in the next step to determine whether the period is open or closed.

2 Now we have completed our prep; we call the function module FI_PERIOD_CHECK in order to determine whether the period is part of a closed period or an open period. Here, we pass the company code contained in the MYBUKRS variable. For I_KOART and I_KONTO, the value of "+" is supplied to the function module. The GJAHR and MONAT are passed the values for year GJAHR and period POPER, both of which we got from the previous function module call.

```
DATA str111 TYPE string. CLEAR str111.
    CALL FUNCTION 'FI_PERIOD_CHECK'
    EXPORTING
      i_bukrs      = MYBUKRS
      i_gjahr      = MYGJAHR
      i_koart      = '+'
      i_konto      = '+'
      i_monat      = MYPOPER
    EXCEPTIONS
      error_period     = 1
      error_period_acc = 2
      invalid_input    = 3
      OTHERS           = 4.
  IF sy-subrc NE 0 AND sy-subrc NE 3.
      MESSAGE 'Period not open' TYPE 'I' DISPLAY LIKE 'E'.
  ENDIF.
```

Here, for the parameters I_KOART and I_KONTO, a value of '+' is specified. The BUKRS along with the fiscal year and period, which we determined in the last step, are also passed via appropriate variables. After the module execution, if the value of the return code (SY-SUBRC) is anything other than 0 or 3, the corresponding posting date is part of a closed period. The appropriate massage is generated.

You may modify the code to suit your particular requirements.

For staying up-to-date
with our latest announcements
regarding ERP magazine
issues and books, subscribe to our
ERPMagazine mailing list
at Google Groups

Learn to Use Advanced Open SQL Features in SAP Reports

Among the latest advancements in the ABAP language, enhancements within Open SQL are of significant importance. In this article, we will see the new features of Advanced Open SQL in action. We will start by reviewing the advantages of Open SQL and Advanced SQL. We will then discuss the main features of the new elements and clauses of Advanced Open SQL and see how all this can be used to achieve code pushdown in HANA so that we can use more efficient programs. Ample coding and illustrations will be provided. While a detailed explanation of Advanced SQL is beyond the scope of this article, we will look at some examples of each new feature.

These are some of the questions this article will address:

- What are some advantages of using the Advanced SQL features?

- What are some of the new features in Open SQL that let you write more efficient, more compact code in newer releases?

- What are some of the syntax errors that may occur in Advanced Open SQL?

Overview of Advanced Open SQL

Advanced Open SQL is very beneficial to developers. Not only is it compact but it also allows us to write more efficient code, as it enables us to push down the application logic to the database, a very useful technique for performance on a HANA system. Prior to the advent of Advanced SQL, SAP developers performed computations in the program on the application server, a clunky and much less efficient method.

Advanced Open SQL has the following advantages:

- Code written in it is database independent.

- It allows the developer to utilize the SAP HANA-specific features of the database.

- It provides more standard SQL-like features for the developer.

Advanced SQL has a number of new features and functions, such as:

- Inline declarations. Inline declarations for variables such as single fields, structures and internal tables are supported within SQL statements.

- String expression. This lets us concatenate a number of fields (with or without literals) while reading from the database.

- Arithmetic expression. This allows us to perform arithmetic calculations with database fields, literal values and program variables.

- CASE expression. This enables us to add conditional checks and specify the corresponding actions to be performed depending on the outcomes.

- Coalesce expression. As the name indicates, this allows us to compare a number of values and return the first nonnull value. This is particularly useful when programming with outer joins. (We will discuss this toward the end of the article.)

Inline Declarations

Advanced Open SQL allows us to use inline declarations. Instead of defining and assigning a data variable for retrieving data before usage, we may carry out an inline declaration for a SELECT statement. We must then make certain changes in the SELECT statement itself for the program to compile correctly.

These changes are:

- Including commas in the list. For example, we must use SELECT FIELD1, FIELD2 rather than SELECT FIELD1 FIELD2.

- Using the escape character @ with each of the data objects and variables (structures as well as internal tables) within the SELECT statement as well as the fields specified via the WHERE clause.

- Making sure that the INTO clause is written right after the field list of the SELECT statement.

Consider the example:
```
select 'Wage Type Text :' && lgtxt as text from t512t into table @data(it_t512t) up to 4 rows
where sprsl eq @sy-langu.
```

Here, we have not used any definition for the IT. We have used a data inline declaration within the SELECT statement, and the statement automatically creates an internal table with field text.

> Note: When including an inline declaration of internal tables with SELECT statements, do not use the INTO... CORRESPONDING addition, as it will generate a syntax error.

We must also use the escape character @ with each variable name and field specified in the WHERE clause.

Once the above statement is executed, the internal table content will be as shown, as in Figure 1.

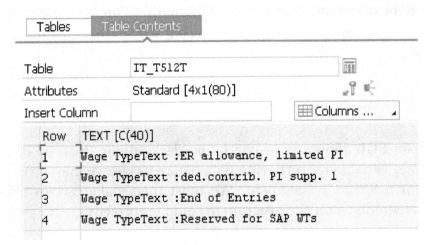

Figure 1: Internal Table Content

It is also important to ensure that when using inline declaration, all variables used in the SELECT statement are escaped using @. If we omit this, a syntax error may result, as shown in Figure 2.

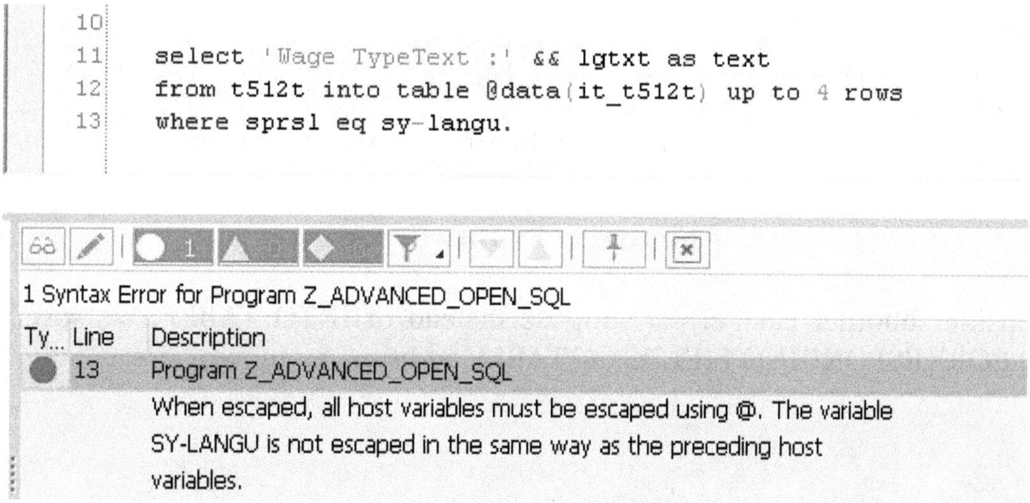

```
10
11     select 'Wage TypeText :' && lgtxt as text
12     from t512t into table @data(it_t512t) up to 4 rows
13     where sprsl eq sy-langu.
```

1 Syntax Error for Program Z_ADVANCED_OPEN_SQL

Ty...	Line	Description
●	13	Program Z_ADVANCED_OPEN_SQL
		When escaped, all host variables must be escaped using @. The variable SY-LANGU is not escaped in the same way as the preceding host variables.

Figure 2: Syntax Error

In this example, the variable SY-LANGU is not escaped using @. Hence, a syntax error is generated.

The correct form of this statement is:

select 'Wage Type Text :' && lgtxt as text from t512t into table @data(it_t512t) up to 4 rows where sprsl eq @sy-langu.

Let us look at another example of syntax errors that may occur if we overlook elements of inline declaration. As already mentioned, we must use commas between table fields while specifying the selected field list.

If we do not use these commas, a syntax error may result. Consider the following:

select 'X' as value1 100 as value2 from t512t into table @data(mydata).

Here we have omitted the comma after the ...value 1. This causes a syntax error, as shown in Figure 3.

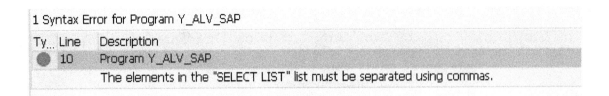

1 Syntax Error for Program Y_ALV_SAP

Ty...	Line	Description
●	10	Program Y_ALV_SAP
		The elements in the "SELECT LIST" list must be separated using commas.

Figure 3: Syntax Error

To consider another easy error, suppose instead of INTO TABLE, we specify the INTO CORRESPONDING FIELDS OF TABLE addition, as shown here:

```
select 'X' as value1   100 as value2
from t512t into corresponding fields of table @data(mydata).
```

In this case, the system issues a syntax error as shown in Figure 4.

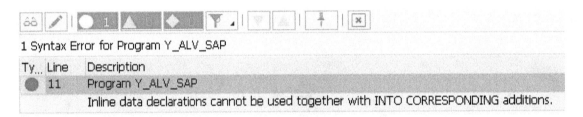

1 Syntax Error for Program Y_ALV_SAP

Ty...	Line	Description
●	11	Program Y_ALV_SAP
		Inline data declarations cannot be used together with INTO CORRESPONDING additions.

Figure 4: Error with Inline Declaration

Literal Values

In Advanced SQL, we can also use literal values within the SELECT field list. These may be both numbers and text values. For example:

```
select 'X' as value1,
       100 as value2   from t512t into table @data(mydata).
```

As you see, we have specified two literal values – one is a single-character literal passed as 'X', and the other is an integer value of 100. After we execute the SELECT statement, the fields VALUE1 and VALUE2 of the internal table MYDATA are filled with 'X' and 100 respectively, as shown in Figure 5.

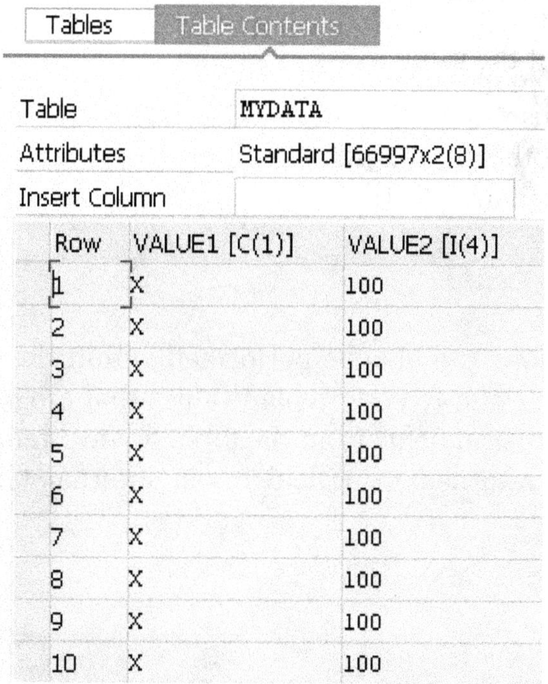

Tables | Table Contents

Table	MYDATA
Attributes	Standard [66997x2(8)]
Insert Column	

Row	VALUE1 [C(1)]	VALUE2 [I(4)]
1	X	100
2	X	100
3	X	100
4	X	100
5	X	100
6	X	100
7	X	100
8	X	100
9	X	100
10	X	100

Figure 5: Contents of MYDATA Table

We can also use literal values to devise existence checks for records in a database table. To illustrate, let us consider an example:

```
data record_exists type abap_bool value abap_false.

select single @abap_true
from t512t where
 SPRSL  eq 'E' and
 MOLGA  eq '01' and
 LGART  eq '/001'      into
@record_exists.

if record_exists eq abap_true.
   write :/ 'Record Found'.
else.
   write :/ 'Record Not Found'.
endif.
```

As you see, we have defined a variable record_exists based on the ABAP_BOOL type and assigned it the value ABAP_FALSE (i.e., ' ').

We can then use ABAP_TRUE in a SELECT SINGLE statement to determine if there is a record in the table T512T based on a SPRSL equal to 'E', MOLGA equal to '01' and LGART equal to '/001'.

String Expression

String operations can also be performed within the Advanced SQL terrain. We can use the && operator to concatenate values that are returned from the database. This may be a number of fields from the table or any literal value. The concatenated value can then be returned in a field of an internal table. Consider our table T512T example:

```
data  it_t512t type STANDARD TABLE OF ty_t512t.
select 'Wage Type Text : ' && lgtxt  as text       from t512t
into CORRESPONDING FIELDS OF
     table @it_t512t up to 4 rows
     where sprsl eq @sy-langu.
```

Here, we have first defined an internal table by the name IT_T512T that contains a single field TEXT based on the type STRING. We are reading the field LGTXT from the database and then using string concatenation && with appropriate text and storing the result in the internal table's field TEXT.

Arithmetic Expression

The new features of the ABAP language support a number of arithmetic functions for creating computational expressions within a SELECT statement. We can use these functions to carry out calculations at the database level. Advanced Open SQL supports a number of operators for such calculations. These are shown in Figure 6.

SQL Function	Result
+	Addition
-	Subtraction
*	Multiplication
ABS(param)	Returns the absolute amount of param.
CEIL(param)	Returns the smallest integer that is not less than param.
DIV(param1, param2)	Returns the whole-number part of the result of the division of param1 by param2.
DIVISION(par1, par2, decimal_ places)	Divides par1 by par2 and returns the result rounded to the specified decimal places.
FLOOR(param)	The highest whole number that is not more than the value of param.
MOD(param1, param2)	The remainder in the result of the division of param1 by param2.

ROUND(param, decimal_places)	This rounds the value of param. If the value of decimal_ places is more than 0, the param value is rounded to the specified number of decimal places.

Figure 6: Arithmetic Functions

Let us now see a working example. Suppose we have a SFLIGHT table that contains flight dates as well as the number of occupied seats and the price for each seat. We can then compute airline income on a particular date, using the SELECT statement shown:

```
select  carrid,connid,
       price * seatsocc  as total_economy_income,
       currency
       into table @data(it_income)
  from sflight
  where fldate eq '19950228'.
```

Here we have used the formula PRICE * SEATSOCC to calculate the total earnings from economy class. This is stored in the TOTAL_ECONOMY_INCOME field of the internal table IT_INCOME, which is declared inline.

The contents of the internal table after the execution of the SELECT statement are shown in Figure 7.

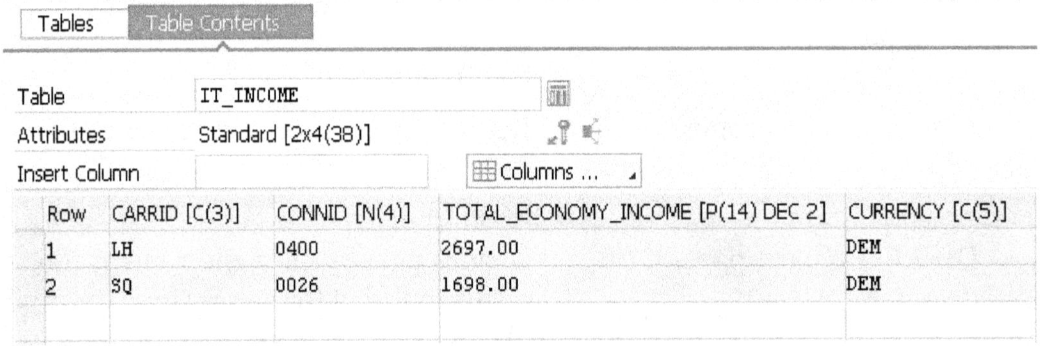

Tables	Table Contents			
Table	IT_INCOME			
Attributes	Standard [2x4(38)]			
Insert Column			Columns ...	
Row	CARRID [C(3)]	CONNID [N(4)]	TOTAL_ECONOMY_INCOME [P(14) DEC 2]	CURRENCY [C(5)]
1	LH	0400	2697.00	DEM
2	SQ	0026	1698.00	DEM

Figure 7: Internal table IT_INCOME

CASE Expression (Conditional Expressions)

Many developers do not yet know that starting from NetWeaver 7.40, ABAP allows us to specify both simple and complex conditions within SELECT statements using CASE expressions. Instead of using IF.. ELSE or CASE.. ENDCASE after a SELECT statement and doing the processing and conditional checks at the application server level, we can now include the condition in the SELECT statement. Let us now see how to do this.

Suppose we are reading the wage-type information from the table T512T. Our requirement is to fetch wage-type code and determine wage-type text according to the following rules:

- Wage type /001 must be specified as 'Wage Type 1'.

- Wage type /002 must have the description 'Wage Type 2'.

- For all other wage types, the text should be returned as 'Unknown'.

If we do not use a CASE expression within our SELECT statement, we need to first read the value of the wage type using a SELECT statement and then use an IF.. ENDIF or CASE.. ENDCASE statement in order to output the correct description. However, using Advanced Open SQL, we can consolidate these steps. Simply writing the statement shown will return the description.

```
TYPES:  BEGIN OF TY_ITAB,
            LGART type t512t-lgart,
            mytext type string,
        END OF TY_ITAB.

DATA ITAB TYPE STANDARD TABLE OF TY_ITAB.

SELECT LGART,
    CASE
        WHEN LGART = '/001' THEN 'Wage Type 1'
        WHEN LGART = '/002' THEN 'Wage Type 2'
        ELSE 'Unknown'
    END AS mytext
FROM T512T INTO TABLE @ITAB.
```

As you see, we have defined an internal table with two fields, LGART and MYTEXT. Within the SELECT statement, we read the field LGART from the table. We then apply the CASE expression to determine the relevant text of the wage type. The text is assigned to the MYTEXT field of ITAB. The output of the code is shown in Figure 8.

Table	ITAB	
Attributes	Standard [20571x2(16)]	
Insert Column		

Row	LGART [C(4)]	MYTEXT [CString]
12	/...	Unknown
13	/0	Unknown
14	/0**	Unknown
15	/0++	Unknown
16	/0--	Unknown
17	/0..	Unknown
18	/00*	Unknown
19	/00.	Unknown
20	/001	Wage Type 1
21	/002	Wage Type 2
22	/003	Unknown

Figure 8: Program Output

In the previous example, we saw a condition based on a single field of the database table. It is also possible to write complicated CASE expressions using a number of fields. Let us see how to do this.

Here, we have a simple requirement involving a table TWB01.

Suppose we need to read the table TWB01, and based on the values of fields BOPNR and BORESVOL, we need to output the BOPNR and the GROUP, according on the following rules:

- When BOPNR is equal to '20FT' and BORESVOL greater than or equal to 1, the group must be '20Ft container'.

- When BOPNR is equal to '40RF' or '0001', the group is 'Non-20Ft container'.

- In all other cases, the group is specified as 'Standard'.

Along with the BOPNR and the GROUP, we also want to output the BORESVOL value.

The code for this is shown here:

```
// Declaration of Internal table

TYPES:  BEGIN OF TY_ITAB,
          BOPNR    TYPE TWBO1-BOPNR,
          GROUP    TYPE CHAR25,
          BORESVOL TYPE TWBO1-
BORESVOL,
        END OF TY_ITAB.
  DATA ITAB TYPE STANDARD TABLE OF
TY_ITAB.


// Get Data
  SELECT BOPNR,
     CASE
        WHEN BOPNR = '20FT' and BORESVOL >= 1
          THEN '20Ft container'
        WHEN BOPNR = '40RF' OR BOPNR = '0001'
          THEN 'Non-20Ft container'
        ELSE 'Standard'
     END AS GROUP,
     BORESVOL
  FROM TWBO1 INTO TABLE @ITAB.
```

Here we have first defined an internal table with two fields, GROUP and BOPNR. We have then written a CASE expression within the SELECT statement, based on the specified rules. The text determined as a result of the CASE expression is returned in the GROUP field of the internal table ITAB.

Coalesce Expression

The Coalesce expression takes a number of values as arguments and returns the first nonnull value. If you have an outer join and a null value might be returned, you can use a Coalesce expression to return a meaningful text value.

Consider a scenario. We have two tables, T512t and T511. T512T is the text tables of all wage types with the appropriate country group (MOLGA), wage type codes and description. The table T511 shows the validity of the relevant wage types, along with other wage-type characteristics. It is possible that T511 may not contain all the wage types mentioned in T512t.

If we have to write a LEFT outer join for these two tables, some of the rows returned may contain null values for T511 fields such as BEGDA, ENDDA and others.

Hence, we will use the Coalesce expression here. The code for this is:

```
select t512t~lgart, lgtxt ,
  COALESCE( begda, 'No Valid Start' )   as validity_start,
  COALESCE( endda, 'No Valid End ' )   as validity_end
into table @data(itab)
from t512t  LEFT OUTER JOIN t511
on ( t512t~molga = t511~molga and
    t512t~lgart = t511~lgart )
where sprsl eq @sy-langu
and t512t~molga eq '01'.
```

This code joins the two tables using LEFT OUTER JOIN. For any null values corresponding to BEGDA and ENDDA, the expression will return text 'No Valid Start' or 'No Valid End' for the internal table fields VALIDITY_START and VALIDITY_END respectively.

The output of the program is shown in Figure 9.

Table	ITAB		
Attributes	Standard [5256x4(114)]		
Insert Column		Columns ...	

Row	LGART [C(4)]	LGTXT [C(25)]	VALIDITY_START [C(14)]	VALIDITY_END [C(14)]
3101	BD61	TxExmptTnsCost EWT TraDat	20040101	99991231
3102	BD62	TxEmp WEnd HJ EWT/DHF CI	No Valid Start	No Valid End
3103	BD70	Tax-Ex. TE Dual Household	20040101	99991231
3104	BD71	Tax-Ex.WTH Dual Household	20040101	99991231
3105	BD80	Tax-Ex. Reimb. Travel Exp	20080101	99991231
3106	BE10	AccomAgre m.Taxab Deduc	No Valid Start	No Valid End
3107	BE11	AccomAgree m.TaxDed. 0215	19000101	20011231
3108	BE11	AccomAgree m.TaxDed. 0215	20020101	99991231
3109	BE20	AccomAgree oTaxDeductions	No Valid Start	No Valid End

Figure 9: Program Output

As you see, once the date is found, it is returned, since it is the first nonnull value encountered. We may then proceed with the processing of the two fields. You may use REPLACE ...REGEX statement to convert the dates into readable format.

For staying up-to-date
with our latest announcements
regarding ERP magazine
issues and books, subscribe to our
ERPMagazine mailing list
at Google Groups